# THE HOUSE & HOME BOOK OF interior design

# THE HOUSE &
# HOME BOOK OF
# interior design

McGraw-Hill Book Company

New York
St. Louis
San Francisco
Auckland
Bogotá
Düsseldorf
Johannesburg
London
Madrid
Mexico
Montreal
New Delhi
Panama
Paris
São Paulo
Singapore
Sydney
Tokyo
Toronto

New York

The editors for this book were Jeremy Robinson and Sue Cymes. The designer was Robert Scharff & Associates. It was set in Chelmsford by Robert Scharff & Associates. Printed and bound by Halliday Lithograph Corporation.

34567890    HDHD    7865432109

Library of Congress Cataloging in Publication Data
Main entry under title:

House & home book of interior design.

Includes Index.
    1. Interior decoration—Handbooks, manuals, etc.

I. House and home. II. Title: Book of interior design.
NK2110.H595    747'.8'8    77-10867
ISBN 0-07-030473-4

# CONTENTS

# Preface

Your home is a very personal place, but it should reflect the world in which you live. And like the rest of the things around us, home interiors are constantly changing. We have noted through the pages of *Housing* (formerly *House & Home*) that certain trends develop in the field of interior design. However, there is a big difference between trends and fads. The latter tend to die out after a few years of popularity, while trends show a definite direction. In this book we hope to show and explain how to decorate your home or apartment—from furniture arrangement to lighting, walls, floors, fabrics—in up-to-date trends, yet still make it a very personal place.

The compilation of this book required the help of many people. For their interior design information as well as for many of the illustrations, we wish to thank the following people and companies. John J. Sullivan, Jr. of Thomasville Furniture Industries, Inc.; Mary B. McClarran of Kittinger Company; Robert L. Ficks, Jr. of Ethan Allen®, Inc.; Patricia G. Mick of Georgia-Pacific Corporation; Norman's of Salisburg; American Drew, Inc.; Roger E. Clark of Richard Le Droff; Nettle Creek Industries; Richard E. Thibaut, Inc.; The Burtley Collection, Ltd.; La Barge Mirrors, Inc.; Nicholas & Stone Company; Nancy E. Christensen of General Electric Company; Plywood Furniture Corporation; Masonite Corporation; Lewis H. Berry of Henredon Furniture Industries, Inc.; Charterhouse Designs, Ronald E. Derk of General Interiors Corporation; Scalamandre; Focal Point, Inc.; Meadowcraft Casual Furniture Company; Weyerhaeuser Company; Spherical Furniture Company; Pulaski Furniture Corporation; Mannington Mills, Inc.; Josephson Company; Amtico Corporation; Mary Osborne of Osborne Associates; and Ted Butler of Supergraphic, Inc.

We would like to especially thank the following for their specific help and assistance in certain areas of the book: Roseann B. Fairchild and The Kirsch Company for permission to use some material appearing in Chapter 4 from their book, *How To Make Your Windows Beautiful; House Beautiful's Home Decorating* and The Hearst Corporation for permission to use the checklist from their Spring 1977 issue that appears in Chapter 14, and Robert K. Marker, of the Armstrong Bureau of Interior Design, and Armstrong Cork Company for permission to use certain materials throughout the book that appeared in their publication, *Armstrong Decorating Ideas For The Active Rooms.* Finally, we would like to thank Barbara A. Pancerella and Mary Puschak of Robert Scharff & Associates for coordinating this entire book project.

To the others who, inadvertently, may have been omitted from the above thank you's, please accept our deep apologies for such omissions.

# HOUSE AND APARTMENT
# design considerations

Whether you're redoing one room or furnishing an entire house, there are basic considerations to be dealt with before you're ready to select the merchandise you need. You must analyze your family's taste and personality traits, decide whether a professional interior designer can help, select a furniture style, plan each room on paper, and anticipate future changes in family living patterns.

In this chapter, we'll take a look at the first two points; in the remaining chapters, we'll look at the others.

**How do you want to live?** What do you and your family like to do? Take a survey of each member of your family and select the home activities which you have in common. These should be featured in your home. All too often the secondary interests are so varied that it's almost impossible to design around them. In such cases, try to create areas for individual activities where each adult and child can pursue individual interests.

Most professional interior designers work out a series of questions to ask their prospective clients, which are devised to help determine where to begin the designing operation. We have included a "typical" questionnaire in Chapter 14. But for now, let's look at some initial questions you should ask yourself.

**Which is everyone's favorite room right now?** Sometimes it takes a bit of living with certain styles and colors to determine what you can really like. Perhaps you decided to try modern when last decorating the living room. Do you find the novelty has now worn off, sending you more and more often to the

**Create areas for individual activities.**

easy chair in the bedroom for evenings when you want to read? It could be that the homelike warmth of your Provincial bedroom is the real you. And what about the rest of the family? They may enjoy the uncluttered simplicity of your living room and be able to lounge in comfort by the hour; if they don't feel at home with the Japanese-style floor pillows and odd-shaped lighting fixtures and complain about the low back on the sofa, the Oriental mood obviously isn't for your family.

**Which of your friends' homes do you enjoy the most?** You may enjoy the company of the Joneses, but find a dinner invitation from them leaves you less enthusiastic than a bid from the Smiths. Maybe it's because sitting on a velvet-cushioned Louis XV chair and sipping demitasse from a fragile cup is not your idea of comfort. The Smiths have a traditional home, too, but their 18th-century English reproductions have the more solid, tailored look that appeals to you. What

you like and dislike about the homes you visit reveals a lot about your true self and what it takes to make you comfortable.

**Do you want a social or a secluded life?** Most of us can't take the constant pace of restaurants and night spots, weekend parties and afternoon gatherings; on the other hand, few people want to retreat completely from others. Usually, we want a bit of both, with emphasis, if any, on seclusion and relaxation, especially in our homes.

It's a great feeling to come home from work or a day of shopping, close the front door, and with that gesture, close out the rest of the world for a short period of time. Of course, if you're at home most of the time, try to keep a room, or even an area of one, in which you can find refreshing privacy. Remember that a house or an apartment may be large in size but small for actual use. Therefore, plan your decorative layout so that you'll have a place to find the escape and relief

3

you need, even though you may prefer your life to be filled with social activities.

For the latter, you'll require space for parties and facilities for making entertaining easy. Such rooms for social activities should be decorated with gay and cheerful colors, and an abundance of small tables and chairs. In cases where space is limited, you can overcome this handicap by utilizing combination or dual-purpose furniture: double-duty chairs, tables, and couches to help conserve space. When selecting the furniture for the social areas of your home, be sure that it can take punishment. Friends are sometimes harder on furniture than children, and occasionally less considerate.

Where comfort, leisure, and seclusion are the major factors, you may have larger furniture—lounging chairs of the utmost comfort are obviously required—ordinarily, fewer pieces are needed. Contemporary or Provincial decor is less likely to be distracting than period, and the colors are more soothing and restrained.

It's not difficult to decide on your life style. Most of us make up our minds fairly early in our adult life. But determining social preferences in terms of home decorating may take a great deal of thought.

**Are you an informal or formal person or family?** In all home decorating, the personal characteristics of the person and family will—or should—ultimately influence the choice of furnishings and decorative theme. For instance, formality often leads to antiques and fine reproductions, and to the styles made famous during the 18th and 19th centuries. Most people who have a predilection toward the past are those who naturally search through stores, talk with dealers, and study books on the subject. You'll be better educated on this subject by reading several books rather than by depending on any single volume for your information.

Incidentally, have you learned the trick of "trying on" the rooms you see in store displays, model homes, and magazine photographs? You can get so much more out of what you see if you acquire the habit of doing a mental exercise when you shop for or read about home furnishings. Don't just look at the dining-room photograph. Imagine the family seated around the table for Sunday dinner. Sometimes the picture will be right, and on other occasions, there will be jarring notes. The furniture may be too informal to do justice to your beautiful linens and china. The high-backed chairs may be wrong when visualized in your low-ceilinged dining room.

**How active are you?** When analyzing your home, keep in mind that some rooms may be classified as *active*, others as *passive*. The places where we do most

An eclectic decor predominates in this living/dining-room area.

A simple contemporary decor requires less up-keep.

4

of our active living—kitchen, dining room, family room, recreation room, and the like—deserve special decorative treatment because they are constantly undergoing heavy use. In a master bedroom used only for sleeping, or a living room in a home that also has a recreation room or a family room, your choice of color schemes and furnishings can be entirely different. Here you don't have to concern yourself with the daily trampling of lively feet, the spilled food and drinks, the carelessness of carefree people. This is the place to use silk-upholstered chairs, delicately proportioned end tables, and nonwashable floor coverings, if you so desire. You can be reasonably impractical without restricting family fun, since most of the time you, the children, and guests will be off somewhere else enjoying yourselves.

It's important, when selecting furniture styles, to honestly answer this question: How hard is your family on household possessions? Certain furniture styles can take more abuse than others, such as big, sturdy, traditional pieces, rather than the more delicate and ornate designs; or contemporary sofas and chairs with separate seat and back cushions that zip off for cleaning and can be replaced inexpensively. If life is quiet and stable at your house, have what you like; if you own a Saint Bernard dog or sharp-clawed cat and have kids who pounce on chairs and all but overturn the tables, make sure the furniture is stronger than

Always suit furniture to your style of living.

An example of theme decoration.

they are.

Another important consideration is how much time you have for housework. If you have a large family and/or work, or have other outside interests, decor that lends itself to easy upkeep is worth considering. Simple contemporary and Provincial furniture pieces are easy to dust and polish; traditional styles with carving and curlicues require more upkeep.

**Do you have a theme?** A theme, as the word implies, is a method of giving character to your home, and it also helps to create atmosphere. When properly handled, a theme can be an excellent short-cut to good decoration. Do you like Early American furniture and Cape Cod houses? Do you tend toward ornate Chippendale, light Sheraton, or heavy Federal? With any of these examples, you're well on your way to the completion of your plan, since most of your choices—furniture, fabrics, and even color—are already made for you.

**Do you have a budget?** A budget is a means of determining what home furnishings you must have in order to achieve what you want in home decoration. After you know this, you can estimate the cost of your plan and divide it, pricewise, into sensible portions which can be spread over a period of weeks, months, or years, without placing you in financial jeopardy. An attractive and well-decorated home is, in this manner, within the reach of the poorest individual, especially when step-by-step planning is behind each move and every purchase.

Sometimes the greatest economy is achieved by choosing quality furnishings that will give years of service—particularly when selecting the basics. When buying such long-term items as flooring, lighting fix-

6

tures, or wall paneling, it pays to spend enough money to assure yourself of good value. It doesn't cost anything to put an adequate amount of time and thought into important purchases; inform yourself of new developments in home furnishing products before making selections.

Also, consider what household furnishings you already have. You may possess a table or two, some chairs, or a sofa that will fit into your new plans. Don't discount them, at least in the beginning. Most decorating plans can be temporarily implemented with a small table, several lamps, considerable paint, and a few slipcovered chairs. Include all your household assets in your planning until you catch up with your budget and the total design of your home becomes apparent—then be ruthless. If possible, discard any object you possess which doesn't fit into your plan, no matter how fond you may be of it or of the person who handed it on to you. After all, you must live with

your home and not with your friends' or relatives' feelings. Sometimes sentiment prevents complete rejection of a piece of furniture. Should this happen to you, consider it carefully and adjust your design accordingly.

In our currently mobile society, many families buy and sell two or three houses before they settle down in a permanent home. This being the case, try to avoid these pitfalls:

1. *"Overcustomizing" your decorating effects.* Even though curved sectionals might well be the very thing for the bay window of your first dwelling, you may have trouble finding the proper spot for them in the rectangular living rooms that follow. Similarly, bookcases, unless designed in small, fit-together modules, might prove too cumbersome for repeated moving.

2. *Buying too hastily.* Furniture and accessories represent a major outlay in almost every household. Take your time and consider each purchase carefully before making it. Allow some budgetary leeway for substitutions or replacements, in case your taste changes or a move to another house makes early choices unusable.

3. *Being influenced too lastingly by temporary surroundings.* For economic and practical reasons, many families live in a Cape Cod or ranch-type bungalow with an eye to purchasing a more stately home in the future. If such is the case in your own family, try to avoid expensive purchases now that won't suit your house of tomorrow.

**Do You Need A Professional Interior Designer?**

Somewhere in the midst of all this soul-searching, the question may come up of whether or not to use a professional interior decorator. The reason so many people have difficulty deciding is that they don't really understand how decorating services operate, what they can do for you, what you should do for yourself—and, most important , how much it all costs.

Qualified interior designers supervise every detail of your decorating project, whether you are redoing one room or furnishing an entire house or apartment. Decorators usually hold one or more consultations with their clients in the beginning, during which they probe like psychiatrists to find out what you're really like—who you are, how you live, what you do, how often you entertain, and what kind of taste you have in furniture, fabrics, colors, and accessories—as well as what you can afford to spend. Gradually, the decorator will put together the type of interior he or she thinks you and your family will like. Although you will

**Existing furniture may fit into new decorating schemes.**

receive suggestions, be shown samples and swatches, and taken to see displays of the furniture the decorator thinks would suit you best, the final decisions rest with you.

A major advantage of working with a decorator is that he or she can help you avoid some of the common, expensive mistakes in judgment that are made every day by amateurs. Few of us can honestly say we've never made a purchase that turned out to be a white elephant—the cocktail table that looked too small in front of the long sofa, the print drapery fabric that seemed more ghastly than gorgeous after it covered an entire wall, or the lamp that wasn't tall enough for a low end table. Even though you may be very positive about what you like and what you don't like, and every purchase you make may be fine by itself, there may be a disappointment or two when you see everything together. A decorator is skilled at coordination, and knows what size the table should be to look right with a particular sofa; what the proper height is for a reading lamp; and which patterns shouldn't be used in large areas. When the decorator does your buying, it's his or her responsibility to follow the rules.

Another advantage the decorator has is access to wholesale showrooms where much of the merchandise is exclusive—that is, it may be sold only through decorators and isn't available to the general public in any other way. This can be helpful in giving your home those extra little touches of originality that distinguish it from others.

If you decide to use the services of a professional decorator, you must first decide exactly how much you want him or her to do. Some interior designers offer different services than others. A few offer consultation only, some will help with the purchasing of the various pieces of merchandise needed, and others will do everything from the basic planning to the completed job. A designer's qualifications can generally be seen in the work he or she has already done. When choosing help, try to visit several decorators, if possible, and see drawings and photographs of their work, and then make your choice accordingly. Membership in the National Society of Interior Designers (NSID) or the American Institute of Interior Designers (AID) is an indication of training and competence. However, there are many good designers who are not members of these organizations.

What does an interior designer charge? Independent interior designers employ various methods of billing a client. A few, for example, charge an hourly rate. However, if you purchase merchandise from the designer, this fee, or at least a portion of it, is credited against your bill.

Another way of billing is for the client to pay retail prices for merchandise and an advance retainer of 10 to 20 per cent of the estimate. This advance percentage paid is then deducted from the final statement. The decorator makes a profit by purchasing items at wholesale prices and selling at retail.

Cost-plus is still another fairly common method of charging for design services. The fee is based on an established percentage of the complete cost of the job. But, except for the cost-plus method of payment, most fees paid to interior designers today come in the form of commissions on the merchandise bought for you. In most cases, you'll be expected to pay shipping charges, sales tax, and any out-of-pocket expenses. But regardless of how the fee is paid, you'll be entitled to a floor plan for each room, a consultation or two about what you should have, and help in selecting the merchandise you need. For special services—trips to your home, an elaborate colored sketch of the planned interior, or help in designing custom cabinets, room dividers, or original window treatments—the professional decorator usually charges by the hour for his or her time.

In addition to decorators who work independently, there are staff decorators employed by department stores who operate in much the same manner. Again, the service is free if you spend the agreed minimum amount for merchandise. You're not limited to selecting everything from the store, for most department store decorators also have access to the trade showrooms not generally open to the public. If you have a favorite store where you feel "at home" and always seem to find what you want, consulting a member of the store's decorating staff may prove to be an ideal arrangement.

For a fee, many decorators will offer you a professional consultation, after which you're free to carry out their suggestions on your own. Department-store decorating services also offer a limited amount of help of this sort to their customers at no charge.

**How An Interior Designer Gets Ideas**
A good interior designer, like a great chef, can easily unharness his or her creative urges and let them run free, but if he or she doesn't have a "well-stocked pantry" or at least access to one, the entire exercise becomes academic—a costly waste of time. To see how professional interior designers obtain many of their ideas, let's see how the various sources of available information are used; many of them are available

8

to you, too.

Today's decorator must keep abreast of the almost daily developments of some 1,000 different sources—from furniture, lighting, carpeting, and wallpaper manufacturers to suppliers of the newest textures and patterns of fabrics; from availability of antiques and replicas to unusual new paint colors and technological breakthroughs in flooring materials and countertops. After all, the interior designer does more than just specify a chair for the den. It has to be a particular chair, covered with a specific fabric (perhaps specially ordered to match a drapery or wallpaper), to comple-

ment and complete the total decor of the room.

A prime source for fresh ideas, one used by virtually every designer, is the "shelter" magazines which showcase some of the best current thinking in the field of interior decor. Certainly a professional designer shouldn't emulate another's work, but from those pages may spring an element or a concept that can well serve as the foundation for a home or apartment interior. Your designer, therefore, should be paying careful attention to publications like *Budget Decorating, Better Homes and Gardens, Southern Living, House Beautiful, House & Garden, Family Cir-*

*cle, and Woman's Day.* Most decorators are great magazine "clippers." That is, they have a complete file of clippings with ideas from a wide range of different sources. Thus, before starting a decorating job in your home, it's a good idea to set up a file and start "clipping."

Keep in mind, however, that the majority of the rooms and homes illustrated are custom-designed for one individual's taste (or else they are room settings created by a department-store decorator to promote merchandise). But some of the styles and design techniques are certainly adaptable to your home, and it

wouldn't hurt to familiarize yourself with current styles and color schemes.

Gift shows, home furnishings shows, and some furniture-store settings can be good sources for design ideas, and most professional interior decorators research them to recharge creative batteries. But remember, most shows of this kind are trying to sell furniture or accessories, or whatever else they are displaying; while you're trying to create a feeling, a design concept, and a life style as embodied in your design.

There are other practical sources for the decorator.

These include illustrated furniture catalogs, fabric samples, brochures on lighting fixtures, and books or samples of wallpaper and paint. A professional decorator keeps all of these sources at his or her fingertips for instant reference. Indeed, they can add up! *House & Home's* decorating consultant, Carole Eichen, has a color-room that contains some 20,000 different fabrics, carpeting, and drapery material samples.

**No need to copy an entire concept, but rather select elements from it to adapt to your own tastes.**

Finally, the first-rate decorator, no matter how busy, will devote a specified amount of time to digging up new sources. An afternoon spent browsing in suppliers' showrooms, talking with representatives, canvassing thrift shops and antique dealers, can spawn a wealth of new ideas. For it is ideas blended with proven techniques that make an interior design good.

**The theme can illustrate a personal hobby or special interest.**

# THE MAGIC OF
# color

**2**

There is a lot of fun and excitement in decorating, but probably no aspect is more pleasurable than working out a color scheme. That's because color is stimulating to the senses. We react to the color around us in various ways, feeling happy when the sun makes all colors brighter, and gloomy when clouds make everything seem dull and gray. While this may seem an elementary fact of nature, people tend to forget it when they are decorating indoors. Many *amateur* interior designers in fact, approach color with too much timidity, relying on "safe" combinations rather than risking color clashes.

Today, there's no need to be intimidated by color. There are a few traditional guidelines that can be followed in selecting colors for homes of various styles. Warm, earthy tones, for example, are popular for ranch-style homes or the Mexican/Spanish motif, while for traditional-style homes, light colors are a good choice. Contemporary homes use a variety of colors from monochromatic whites and beiges to earthy browns accompanied by heavy textured fabrics. In a country French-style decor, warm, almost pastel shades of green, yellow, and tan are found most often. While these are the basic trends, the final choice of color is left to the individual, and there are many colors that can be used. No one is bound by the old color rulebook anymore. In fact, there are no longer rules which say you must use a specific color with a certain style of furniture.

For example, red, white, and blue, long associated with Colonial styles, can now be combined very effectively in a contemporary motif as well. Yellow is often considered a traditional color, but gray and yellow contemporary fabrics go exceptionally well with chrome and glass in contemporary-theme homes. As little as 10 or 20 years ago, this freedom and boldness was unheard of, and the interior design profession would not have even given a thought to such combinations. White, beige, peach, and maroon were "in" colors for walls and ceilings.

Also years ago, you would never have mixed, say, pink and orange; the old color rulebook said it clashed. But, thanks to artists and fashion designers and the rebellious young, who were willing—no, eager—to defy the rules, our eyes have become accustomed to all sorts of mad, wonderful combinations. They're not only acceptable—they're marvelous!

Now that we've made the point for freedom in color choice, let us give you the tried-and-true "rules" of using color—basic facts that you should know about how color works. It's not that you need be bound by these rules; only that you may be guided. Once you get into the swing of using color, you may soon want to go off into untried worlds. Until then, look with assurance to these timeless truths.

### What Is Color?

Color, per se, is not hard to understand. Look at the color wheel shown here. This is based on pigment colors, those you see in printing, in printed fabrics, in wallcoverings, and in art and painting generally. The three main categories of color are as follows:

**Primary Colors.** The longest extended slices on the

12

color wheel show the three primary colors—red, yellow, and blue. They're called primary because all the other colors come from combinations of these three colors.

**Secondary Colors.** Mix any two primary colors and you get the secondary colors:

Orange (Red & Yellow)
Violet (Red & Blue)
Green (Blue & Yellow)

**Tertiary Colors.** All of the other six colors on the wheel are called tertiary, or intermediate colors. They are a mixture of the primary colors plus an adjacent secondary color. Thus:

Yellow Orange (Yellow & Orange)
Yellow Green (Yellow & Green)
Blue Green (Blue & Green)
Blue Violet (Blue & Violet)
Red Violet (Red & Violet)
Red Orange (Red & Orange)

Color has three dimensions: the *hue*, distinguishing one color from another—such as red, green, blue, etc.; the *value*, denoting lightness or darkness; and the *tone* or *intensity*, which is the brightness or dullness.

These hues, values, and intensities can appear to change when different ones are used together. Two or more light values combined afford little contrast; nor will darker values in combination provide much interest. But, when a light value is used with a dark, the light appears lighter while the dark appears darker. White is the lightest of all colors, and values range from it through varying gradations of gray to black. Colors that are nearer white in value are called *tints* and colors that are close to black in value are called *shades*.

Intensities or tones also have similar effects. A brightly upholstered chair will appear brighter and will stand out when used with a carpet of dull color, as it will produce a spot of interest. In contrast, a few dull-colored pieces of furniture will sink into the background if the room contains brighter-colored rugs, draperies, and other furnishings.

Contrasting or opposite hues will emphasize one another. Red with green will make the red look redder and the green appear greener; while similar hues together will seem to change the hues. For example, if a red is used with red-purple, the red will appear more orange, while the red-purple will take on a bluish tone.

There are many ways of combining colors for interest. Related color schemes such as reds, purples, and blues together can produce very pleasing effects.

The basic color wheel with a three-dimensional projection of the attributes of color—hue, value, and intensity as shown in their relation to one another. The circular band represents the hues: G-green, B-blue, P-purple, R-red, and Y-yellow. The upright center axis is the scale of value. Paths leading from the center indicate color intensity.

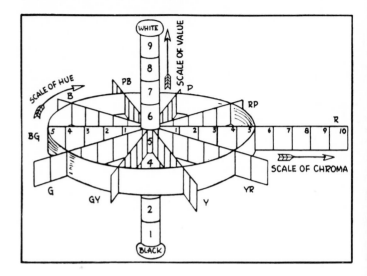

Contrasting hues, such as blues with oranges, can also be combined to give more vibrant results.

Some people enjoy excitement. Warm colors such as yellow, orange, and red are exciting because they are associated with things like sunshine, fire, heat, and even blood. Warm colors tend to "advance," and a predominantly warm-colored wall will seem to come forward. They are especially effective in rooms that are on the east or north side of a house, because light entering from those directions seems to be a cool light. The warm colors and cool light complement each other and make the room seem cozier and warmer.

Cool colors are those associated with water, verdure, and the sky—blues, greens, and violets. These tend to "recede," and under most conditions, light, cool-colored walls will created an illusion of greater space. They are good choices for rooms on the south and west side of the house, since these areas receive a lot of sunlight all year around. Theirs is a cooling effect in the warm-light areas, another complementary association.

Black, white, gray, and brown—and the tones of the latter two, known as griege and beige—are not considered to be colors so much as *neutrals*. In practice, they are the "no-color" colors, which are used with other colors to modify them or to contrast with them. But they are far from being negative. As you work with color, you will find that all colors are influenced by the company they keep. This is particularly true of the tints, shades, and so-called neutral colors. A juxtaposition of two muted colors, such as a gray and a tan, will bring out latent greens, lavenders, and pinks you did not see before.

matic color scheme, the interest of the room comes through by using a variety of textures and patterns.

**Analogous or Related.** Because it's the easiest color scheme to work with, an analogous scheme is the one that enjoys the greatest popularity at the present time. It is based on two or three colors, such as yellow, yellow orange, and red orange, that lie close to each other on the color wheel, with "relief" provided by tints and shades of the same that have been tinged with adjacent greens or vermilion. The analogous color scheme is restful and refreshing also, and the colors are more interesting because of their variations in intensity and value. It is the kind of color scheme that is easily changed; a slight shift of emphasis here and there is all that is necessary to completely change the character of the room.

**Complementary or Contrasting.** This scheme, which is rapidly coming into favor, uses colors that are opposite each other on the color wheel—blue and orange, red and green, yellow and violet. One color is usually a primary color and the other a secondary color. Using such contrasting colors will give a lively and vibrant room, but it is a color scheme that must be used with caution. One color should always dominate, with the others being primarily dramatic accents. The "shock" impact of a complementary color scheme can be softened by selecting unexpected shades and tints of the two colors. That is, a vivid color and its complement can be quieted, if you prefer, by graying them, or reducing their values. Employing a pair of opposites in this manner means that there will be both cool and warm colors in a room, which makes a mutually complementary association. A complementary color scheme tends to make a room seem smaller.

**Accented.** This is a combination of adjacent, related, or analogous colors—call them what you will—accented by a bold touch of color from the opposite side of the wheel. An example would be a scheme ranging through a number of strong, soft, and grayed yellows, spiked with purple or violet.

There are also other color schemes, such as *triad* and *split-complementary* that you can adapt from the color wheel, but the four suggested above are the easiest to visualize and to carry out.

In whatever basic scheme you use do not forget the neutrals: black, white, the grays, and browns—to which you might add metallic gold and silver. Since they will appear, of themselves, in the wood and metal of your furnishings, they must at all times be considered for the part they play in the total effect. If you wish, the neutrals can constitute a fifth, and very

Colors also have visual weights. Dark and bright appear heavy, while light or dull seem to weigh less. Remember that a dominant color is the one that "controls" a room, while the others are accents.

### Basic Color-Scheme Planning

Successful decorating often depends on how well the total effect is anticipated. Here are four types of schemes that professional decorators have in mind when they start to plan a job. They are no guarantee of perfect results, but they do make an unwieldy subject easier to handle.

**Monochromatic.** This scheme is built around one color, using it somewhere in its full intensity, and then varying it with a number of shades and tints of the same color. For example, in a monochromatic scheme of yellow, the range could be from dark shades of gold, through clear yellows, to light, pale-yellow tints. A monochromatic color scheme can be restful, create a feeling of spaciousness, and provides a good background for art objects, collections or similar decorations. But generally, when employing a monochro-

sophisticated color scheme of their own! But usually they must be more or less just "accepted," and played up or played down by the colors you combine them with. Incidentally, some black and white is an asset to almost any color scheme, but too many and indefinite neutrals, used with stronger colors, tend to compromise a color scheme and make it look confused or merely drab. It is best to think of any neutral as a distinctive note of color, whether it is the fieldstone of a fireplace, or a hardwood floor.

## What Color Does

Color excites, motivates, persuades. Color can also offend, shock, and depress. But so much nonsense has been written about the psychology of color that it is time to get down to cases. It would be hard to improve on the common expressions we use every day, to wit:

I'm in the pink (I feel great)

I feel blue (I'm sad)
Green with envy (jealous)
Born to the purple (blue-blooded, aristocratic)
Red with rage (angry)
Blue with cold (far from warm!)
True blue (honest)

It is interesting to note that the word "blue" is used, above, in four different contexts: psychological, sociological, physiological, and moral. This should be fair warning that generalizations about color are seldom objective. In popular opinion, cool colors are associated with sadness and melancholy, warm colors with gaiety and high spirits. Does this explain why red is the color both of love and anger? Both emotions are intense. As to which kind of people prefer what kind of color, we are on extremely uncertain ground. People with dark hair and "outgoing" people are said to like reds and the warmer colors best, while those with blond hair and fair skin, supposedly more in-

troverted, prefer blues and the cooler colors. Needless to say, this would be hard to prove, for anyone can immediately think of several exceptions, including perhaps oneself. The truth of the matter may be that we subconsciously favor the colors we believe are "becoming" to use and that these, for that very reason, affect us emotionally.

In his poem, "Raphael," John Greenleaf Whittier wrote, "The tissue of Life to be / We weave with colors all our own..." The highly personal nature of the whole subject of color psychology could not be put more concisely. The colors we choose to wear are, by and large, the right colors to have around us if we are to be in harmony with our environment. Aside from this basic consideration, special rooms demand special colorings, just as special occasions call for special clothes. This brings us to the brink of color symbolism, but we will mention it only in passing. A subject in itself, symbolic color enters into the decoration of public places more than it does the home. Where it is most noticeable—and differs so widely—is in the customs of national groups of people. For example, to the Chinese, white is the color of mourning, of endings; to us it is the color of weddings, of beginnings. It is also the symbol of purity.

If your spirits are lifted by bright and bold colors in your wardrobe, chances are you will react even more positively to a whole roomful of vibrant hues. You may have seen and admired a family room done completely in hot pink, or a white-floored, black-walled study relieved only by zebra stripes. If you would like to try your own hand at such dramatic approaches, here are some pointers to guide you:

*Look to the experts* and study each detail. It is usually the subtle touches that give such striking rooms a look of fiesta rather than fiasco.

*Break the visual impact* with pattern or texture. A sofa upholstered with red-on-red brocade is not nearly so flaming as a sofa in bright red satin.

*Use toned-down shades* of intense colors, particularly when you are striving for a monochromatic look in a vivid hue. Whereas a totality of mustard-yellow might be unbearable, a step or two down the color scale might render such a room not only tolerable, but highly satisfactory. Proceed with caution, evaluating the effect of one wall before you proceed with all four.

*Use correlated shades* of the same color to add interest to a monochromatic scheme and provide relief for the eye.

## Color As A Tool

Color is a decorator's tool. In the same way that a

carpenter uses his saw, you can use color to create the effects you wish.

**Use Color To Create Visual Changes.** When it comes to choosing specific tones, you will want to keep in mind the optical illusions that can be achieved with color. As mentioned previously, bright or deep colors come forward; white, neutrals, and pastels retreat. Keeping it light is almost mandatory where small room dimensions are a problem. White or a very light tint of a color can really push back the walls, creating the illusion of space. In larger rooms that are too long and narrow, end walls might be painted in a deeper color to bring them forward and thus cut down on the ratio of length to width. A high ceiling, too, can be brought down with a color deeper than the walls; a low ceiling can be made to appear higher if painted lighter.

**Unify Colors To Minimize Architectural Defects.** An unattractive jog, exposed pipe, or window frame can be made less conspicuous by painting it the same color as the surrounding walls. Unattractive furniture, too—the old-fashioned bulky chest or overstuffed chair you can't afford to throw out just yet—can be minimized by painting or slipcovering it so it will "disappear" into the wall.

**Rely On Color To Brighten Dark Areas.** Perhaps your problem is paneled walls. Many of us select a certain house simply because we can't resist the warm wood tones of a paneled living room or den. Once we've moved in, however, we may find that rooms that looked cozy and inviting on a bright spring afternoon appear rather dull and depressing on a winter's day. Use color to lighten, brighten, and heighten such a room—light floors and ceilings, sunny-toned slipcovers and draperies, and furniture in light-toned woods or paint colors. If you have no budget for major furniture changes, try adding a white marble top to your coffee table, lacquering or antiquing a too-dark chest or cabinet, or stretching a buttercup-yellow shelf across one end of the room. Lighting, too, is a corrective feature. Substitute translucent

A light-colored bed spread against a darker wall background draws attention to an attractive headboard.

shades that give an over-all glow for opaque or too-dark ones. Use sheer window treatments to admit more natural light, and pictures matted with wide white borders. For a detailed discussion on the effects of various window treatments, see Chapter 4, pages 83 to 90.

**Use Contrasting Colors To Give Emphasis.** You may want to show off certain features of the room, such as a window with a good view, handsome wood moldings, or a fine piece of furniture. Paint the window frame a different color from the wall, stain the wood moldings, and upholster the chair in a fabric that contrasts with the walls and floor.

**Use Color For Correlation.** Open-plan homes, with one area merging into the next, offer particular problems and special challenges. The ideal is to "marry" each room to its mate without committing yourself to utter sameness throughout the house. Color affords an excellent solution. Reverse your color scheme as you proceed from area to area. If your living room is done in moss green with accents in bitter lemon, tie in your dining alcove with bitter lemon as the primary or background color, and soft green repeated in chair seats and decorative accessories.

### Where To Find Inspiration

No matter how much you love color, it may be hard for you to visualize the finished room done in the colors of your choice; or, you may be simply unable to narrow down the spectrum to about three colors. Yet, when you see a well-executed combination of colors, you know immediately that this is what you would like to have in your own home. Then why not copy from a plan that is already laid out for you?

"Stealing" ideas from interior designers, artists, and others is no crime. When you steal from a picture in a book or magazine, a department store display, or a home-furnishings-show model room setting, you are in fact doing exactly what the creators expect. Just remember that, as an individual, you are bound to have some differences of opinion with the original designer. Never assume that because something was done by a professional, it should not be altered somewhat by an amateur. Some of the most beautiful homes are created by those who know how to use the ideas of others, but with little adaptations here and there that tailor the final product to their own personalities. Here are some likely sources to get you started on a color scheme:

**Start With A Pattern.** Very often, a closer look at a pattern that strikes your fancy will reveal the makings of a complete color scheme. You may have seen a wallpaper or fabric pattern featuring pink and red roses on a white background. Why not follow through with white walls, pink-and-white floor covering in a subtle striated patterned fabric, and furniture antiqued with pink and white spray paint? Add a touch or two more of the red in toss pillows and lampshade border. You might also build a room around the colors in a flooring pattern—the varied monochromatic tones of a terrazzo or marbleized vinyl will impart a simple elegance to a hall, bedroom, or family room; the brightness of a patterned linoleum can inspire you to plan a more colorful kitchen. If you like frequent changes of color scheme, select a subtle pattern in a neutral tone. This will give you the freedom you need to switch to any combinations of colors you want in paint, fabrics, and other less permanent furnishings.

**Adapt From A Model Room Setting.** The word to stress here is adapt, for model room settings are not places where real people engage in everyday activities. Sometimes a color scheme is deliberately dramatized in order to attract attention, whereas a subtler version would be easier on the eyes for a room in constant use. Practicalities, too, are often overlooked in display rooms, since there is no need to worry about upkeep. You may see a marvelous room in dazzling white, black, and red, with the most outstanding feature a white-upholstered sofa on a black-and-white

checkerboard floor. White will never do as an upholstery fabric for your family room, but if you are buying slipcovers, a black-and-white print in a washable fabric might be a good substitute. If you are buying a new sofa, you can choose one of the washable plastics simulating white leather. If checkerboard flooring is too high style for the room, substitute a marble, pebble, or stone texture with a white background, adding black or black-and-red feature strips.

**Start With A Favorite Color.** If there is one color for which the family has a preference, this may be the best place to start. Either use several tints and shades of this color, ranging from light to dark, to build a monochromatic scheme; or combine it with some other color that makes a particularly good mate. If blue is the chosen color, for example, you can do the entire room in blue, or blue with white. If you prefer a more varied scheme, you might choose to merge blue with green—one of the loveliest and most relaxing combinations.

**Borrow From Nature.** Unexcelled in beauty are the color schemes to be found in the great outdoors—a blue sky with white clouds meeting a forest of green; the multicolored splendor of gold, red, yellow, and brown autumn leaves; or even your own garden of spring flowers. What you appreciate most out of doors is often a clue to the colors you would enjoy liv-

**Do-it-yourself supergraphics allow the expression of bold sweeps of color.**

ing with at home.

**Borrow From Famous Artists.** A lovely, serene painting may have in it just the colors you need for a traditional or contemporary room—and if the artist lived at the same time as your period furniture was designed, you have a team. Inexpensive prints of masterworks are sold in book stores and museums. As for contemporary art, many works are studies in color and form. The right choice of a modern painting may prove to be not only the inspiration for your color scheme, but the focal point of your contemporary room.

### Your Final Color Choice

Frequently it's a good idea to change the pace and color scheme from room to room. The mood of a kitchen should differ from that of a living room. In adjoining rooms, unite the schemes with the same carpet or wall color.

If you're redecorating, start with colors you have. If the sofa stays, pick up a color from its upholstery for walls. Choose one from the wallpaper for a new drapery; or try a shade from the carpet or slipcovers. It will hold your room together.

Once you have decided on the colors you want and how much area is to be covered by each, all that remains is to promise yourself that you will work with swatches from start to finish, not making any purchases until the final swatch is in and evaluated. Remember that bright colors and patterns are more so in large doses. That little paint chip in the catalog is the biggest illusion of them all, for the color you see in miniature will look entirely different when it covers a room. It's well worth the time and money invested to buy half a yard of fabric and bring it home to throw over the sofa, or to paint a good-sized section of a wall and let it dry overnight before proceeding further. A yellow that seems demure as a buttercup when it's one-inch square may be too hot to handle when spread all over the room.

After you have gathered samples of your flooring, paint colors, or wallpaper, upholstery and curtain fabrics, take a good, long look at them in relation to each other. The best way to do this is by incorporating them in your floor plan, snipping off bits of fabric and placing them on the outlines that represent your sofa, chairs, and windows. With crayon, fill in the floor area in colors as close to the original as you can get. Then place paint or wallpaper samples around the perimeter. Using the three-dimensional floor plan suggested in Chapter 14, page 159, will make it even easier to plot and visualize your color scheme.

### The Effects of Light on Color

Lighting is of two types, natural and artificial. In natural daylight we say that we see colors as they really are. Scientifically true or false, it is still the most practical and universal standard—the only reasonably sure way to judge color. But what good does this do if the colors we choose will be seen, most of the time, under artificial lighting? Fortunately incandescent light does not radically change colors. Standard incandescent light, as our eyes perceive it, simply deadens most colors, making them appear to be seen through slightly amber-colored glasses. That is, the light from an incandescent-filament bulb is warm in color quality and imparts a friendly, homelike feeling to interiors. Under this light source, the warm colors (the oranges, reds, browns, etc.) are enhanced, while the cool colors (the blues and greens) are subdued. Generally, when the over-all atmosphere of a room is on the warm side, the full values of the warm colors will be acceptable when filament bulbs are used. While

many of the blues and greens in fabrics, flooring, countertops, wallcoverings, and paint will be muted or slightly changed in color, there is not a general consciousness of these shifts.

There are also tinted incandescent bulbs in yellow, pink, aqua, green, and blue. They are recommended for locations where the specific effect of a warm or cool mood or atmosphere is desired. In general, tinted light subtly accents like colors, and subdues complementary colors. Yellow and pink bulbs produce a warm-colored tint of light that intensifies warm coloring in home furnishings; aqua, green, and blue bulbs give emphasis to cool colors in a decorative scheme. If desired, the appearance of a color scheme can be changed by using yellow and pink bulbs to subdue cool colors, and aqua, green, and blue bulbs to tone down warm colors. Seasonal changes can be made without resorting to more complex or expensive methods to achieve the color appearance of coolness in summer and warmth in win-

ter. In rooms which have neutral color schemes, tinted bulbs can subtly create quite a different atmosphere. The addition of color to incandescent bulbs will, however, reduce the light output compared to that of either the inside-frosted or white-coated bulbs. It is suggested that to compensate for the reduced light output, tinted bulbs of the next higher wattage be used, if approximately equal lighting results are desired.

While incandescent-filament bulbs cause few problems with color, gas or vapor-filled lighting fixtures wreak havoc on them (and complexions). Of these, the best-known are neon lighting, which is largely confined to signs, and fluorescent lighting, which is fairly standard equipment in commercial and industrial installations. Fluorescent lights come in considerable variety, depending upon the vapor used and the color of the glass tubing. But, as they work on an ultraviolet principle, it is obvious that the colors that will be seen under them must be selected "ultra"-carefully. Today, however, the skilled interior designer can work successfully with a palette of seven "whites" to create the atmosphere desired. Listed below are the seven whites used most in interior work, with a description of the color characteristics of each.

*Deluxe Warm White* (WWX). Creates a warm atmosphere and blends well with incandescent bulbs. Enhances most colors in floor coverings, furniture, fabric, and paint.

*Delux cool White* (CWX). This fluorescent color gives the most accurate color rendition of all fluorescent tubes, but its cool light is quite different in appearance from the mellow, yellowish incandescent lighting usually found in the home. It's best for kitchen use where cool colors predominate in the decoration, and where a cool atmosphere is desired.

*Warm White.* A light which will blend with incandescent lighting, but somewhat adversely affects both warm and cool colors.

*Cool White.* Light which produces a cool atmosphere, but dulls warm colors and intensifies cool colors.

*White.* Compromise between warm white and cool white; slightly dulls the appearance of warm colors.

*Daylight.* Very blue-white light seldom used in homes because it grays complexions, dulls warm colors, and creates a very cold atmosphere.

**Consider the effect of different types of lighting on your color scheme.**

*Soft White.* Pinkish white light that emphasizes reds and pinks, but has a tendency to gray cool colors.

The choice of fluorescent tubes now becomes simply a matter of deciding first whether a warm or a cool atmosphere is desired for the room. Therefore, when the room's atmosphere and color rendition are of prime importance, the corresponding warm or cool tube to improve color rendition would be chosen; if light output is the most important requirement, the warm, warm white, or cool white tubes will serve.

All white fluorescent tubes look alike when unlighted. The name of the white color (which varies among manufacturers), as well as the wattage of the tube, is printed on the glass tube at one end. Fluorescent tubes in color—red, pink, blue, and gold—may be used for a decorative accent, or combined to produce a desired blending of colors.

## Line, Form, Texture, and Pattern

As we can see, color has power. It can be bright to attract our attention, or passive to allow our gaze to focus elsewhere. Because it has this power to persuade, it is obviously an important consideration in interior design. But, there are several other items— line, form, texture, and pattern—that go hand in hand with color to complete a room scheme.

**Line.** Line may move in any direction: up and down, or in diagonals to form zigzags. Lines form the boundaries which define the shape or silhouette; and within these silhouettes, lines divide the whole into

**Soft, filtered light produces a cool, relaxed atmosphere.**

parts or spaces. Lines can also be used to decorate, form patterns, to create illusions, or express emotions.

Lines can be thick or thin, long or short, straight or curved, clear-cut or fuzzy. Long, slender, vertical lines placed close together give a feeling of dignity, stability, and height. Curved, flowing lines express grace and rhythm, as a bird in flight or the ripples in a stream.

How does this apply to interior design? A room which is too low can be given the feeling of height by strong vertical lines, such as contrasting strips between cabinets and built-ins, or striped wallpaper. It is the old idea of "verticals heighten, and horizontals widen." Yet, if the designer is knowledgeable, a series of narrow vertical lines close together can create just the opposite effect—widen instead of heighten.

Vertical lines are also strong, like a person standing; horizontal ones suggest rest. Applying these values to the open-shelf concept, horizontal shelf lines create a restful effect in rooms—perhaps even suggesting the

**(Top) A predominance of light colors together with a wall of sunlight creates a warm feeling. (Bottom) Finely detailed patterns give a delicate effect.**

22

area itself is relaxed and is a place to relax in. Green plants of varying size and fullness always add softness to the many straight lines and hard surfaces of an area such as a kitchen, and when placed on open shelves, they are especially great in juxtaposition with the glass walls of modern apartments.

**Form.** Form is the mass or the volume, and the shape of the object. Each item displayed potentially adds decorative pleasure according to its shape and size.

Visual form is closely allied with the apparent weight of the object. While actual weight is important, frequently it is the apparent weight which is the deciding factor as to whether an object successfully goes with the design. A shape strongly contrasting with its background will have more visual or apparent weight than one which is similar. Thus, as applied to kitchen decorating, for example, a large white refrigerator might be too dominant for a room having dark walls and cabinets; but, with light walls, the refrigerator might assume less importance. Conversely, the refrigerator could be darkened and the same desired result would occur in relation to the dark walls.

Another aspect of form that is important is the difference between mass form and skeleton form. A large item which has the visual appearance of a solid box, with the structure within, is an example of a mass form. A mass form frequently suggests weight, apparent if not actual, and may require conpensatory treatment, such as color or surface decoration. The above reference to the refrigerator is such an example.

The second type of form is called the skeleton form.

**This sofa's bumpy surface texture is appropriate for its large size.**

A group of open shelves, a wire hanging planter, or a room divider, all having their structure revealed, would be classified as skeleton. These forms will be very linear in quality and will generally have less apparent weight. However, these forms can be just as dominant visually as the mass form, and it is important to learn to use both of them in appropriate ways. A skeleton form can occupy as much space as a mass form, but it usually defines, rather than encloses, space; consequently, it may appear to be smaller than it actually is.

**Texture and Pattern.** All forms and surfaces have texture—they give a tactile sensation when touched. They feel smooth, rough, jagged, slick, soft, hard, warm, or cold. Some have a regularity of surface; others are varied with no apparent order to the surface. But touch is not the only sense which is affected. Sight also plays an important part in the study of textures. What of the surface which has a pattern on it rather than in it? Does this not give an equal sensation? Yes, frequently it does.

There are two kinds of texture. One, the actual texture, which is the tactile quality of a surface. The second is a simulated texture or applied pattern, which does not affect the tactile quality, but does affect the visual quality. The eyes "feel" the surface rather than the fingers. Often both texture and pattern are combined, and further aesthetic tendencies are established.

All forms in the rooms of the house have texture and pattern—fabrics, stone, wood, glass, metal, plaster, brick, china, plants, and plastics. The surface of a form has a great deal to do with its inherent qualities of weight and density. A form will take on more importance when its surface contrasts greatly with the surface texture and/or pattern of its background. In fact, frequently the size or form is visually changed by the use of texture and pattern. For example, a large, plain-surfaced form might almost disappear against a plain-textured background, as might a pattern against a pattern. Sometimes, however, a boldly patterned large form will be visually broken into smaller parts and can be camouflaged, almost appearing as a group of small forms.

Heavy, bulky, thick, or fuzzy textures in fabrics, when used on a large piece of furniture, will definitely increase the apparent size, but when used on small delicate furniture, the piece will seem to be overburdened by such weight, and consequently, will appear even smaller and overpowered by the covering.

Shiny textures reflect light. Because of this, the shape or form underneath will stand out. Shiny textures will intensify the color, also. The same fabric will appear brighter in satin than in crepe.

Crisp-looking fabrics, especially if dull in color, are good camouflages. They have a tendency to hide the shape underneath because the fabric does not cling and define. Crisp fabrics also give a feeling of neatness and order, but they will not fall easily into folds. If draperies are made of fabrics that are too crisp, they may jut out in an awkward position. Softer, more flexible fabrics are ideal for draped designs; but if the fabric is too thin or sleazy, it will eventually hang limp and lifeless.

Nubby textures will soil more quickly; however, they will not show the soil as readily as smooth fabrics, particularly if they contain a mixture of colors. Actually, no hard and fast rules regulate the use of a mixture of textures. We must become sensitive to harmony in our combinations. For instance, smooth woods can be used with rough brick, and soft velvets can be combined with crepes, which appear to be hard. But in each case, these contrasting textures should be tied together harmoniously. Unity of color may be the solution, or perhaps, rhythmic lines can draw the two together. At times, it might be necessary to introduce a third intermediate texture as a transition from one to another. A nubby chair cover may have a smoother cording around the cushions which would help to tie it to the smoothness of the wood frame.

In general, it is always safe to combine similar textures, but carefully considered contrast in textural quality can enhance both surfaces. Rough wood, fieldstone, and homespun fabrics are quite compatible, but often, by adding plate glass, chromed steel, or other hard surfaces, all the surface qualities are immeasureably enhanced. Use contrasting textures for variety where contrasting colors or patterns might destroy unity. This is especially true when a very lim-

**(Opposite page) The buffet is a good example of mass form.**

ited color scheme might tend to be dull and drab. Finally, remember that all surfaces have texture and must be considered in the total design, not just the surface treatments of the major items.

Pattern, like color, can be an eye-catching accent or a dominant factor in a room. The more you use, the more it dominates. In picking a pattern, relate it to room size—small patterns in small rooms, large ones in large rooms.

## Five Basic Principles of Design

The first principle can be expressed as *unity with variety*. The proper use of line, form, texture, and color are considerations that can generally make a major improvement in the appearance of any room, but a sense of order is also needed for an aesthetically pleasing design. Order can easily be achieved by unity of all parts, but if all parts are exactly alike, monotony or boredom may be the result. Therefore variety must be introduced for interest.

The second principle to be considered is *balance*. An experienced interior designer is one who knows just how much variety in color, texture, or line is needed to produce a pleasing effect. But if there are several variations of one of these components, then the others should remain more constant in order to retain the harmony of the whole. For example, if several colors, or many intensities and values of one color, are desired, then closely related textures and lines could hold these color variations together.

The third principle to remember is the need to maintain one *center of interest*, instead of many strong features vying for attention. To minimize the confusion that might occur when using a number of colors, textures, and types of lines, one dominant idea should be emphasized. In a room, this could be an unusual piece of furniture occupying a prominent place, a lovely picture on the wall which is first seen when entering the room, a fireplace with logs burning in it, or an attractive centerpiece on the table. That is, one feature should be emphasized by the use of color, line, or texture importance. But, this point of emphasis might be too shocking if it is so different or unusual in any of those elements that it stands out by itself.

Any method that will lead the eye to the center of interest will produce *rhythm,* the fourth principle that should be considered when creating good design. You can do this in many ways, such as grouping smaller or less important articles of furniture or accessories in an attractive arrangement near the main piece; repeating the color of the main piece in other parts of the room to lead the eye to the dominant point; or by using a gradation of color from light to dark, or dull to bright, to carry the eye to the darkest or the brightest area. Gradation of size is also effective.

The fifth principle, the use of good *proportion*, or scale, should never be overlooked when you are choosing the sizes and shapes to be combined. The scale of sizes and shapes within a room should be in relation to the whole. For example, a large, heavy piece of furniture will dwarf a small room. On the other hand, tiny, insignificant-sized items will look ridiculous in a large room.

The knowledge and the use of all these principles in handling the elements of line, texture, and color will not necessarily produce beautiful results, however. Imagination, understanding, and personal taste must be developed to a point where the combining of these elements becomes a natural skill, instead of a maneuvered or set pattern of arrangements.

Skylights and curved windows such as those shown here are popular innovations in modern architectural design.

(Below) Three examples of wall treatments: knotty pine plywood paneling; fabric-backed vinyl wall-covering; and an adaptation of a document pattern dating back to Salem of the 1600s.

(Above, top left and right) Screen-printed vinyl wallcovering in the kitchen and bedroom; (bottom) entire bathroom done in attractive low-maintenance, glazed mosaic tiles.

(Above) Diagonally patterned wood-grain paneling.

(Left) The floor covering blends harmoniously with the natural wood hues of the walls and furniture.

(Below) Five more varieties of wallcoverings: (top left) weave design silk-screened wallpaper; (top center) is a rough-textured acrylic finish; (top right) decorative brick for the kitchen; (bottom left) paneling with rustic look of old barn wood; and (bottom right) a wall mural of giant sunflowers.

An assortment of floor coverings: (above) light-colored shag carpet; (left) for a uniquely styled floor arrangement, a Berber-look carpet with a nubby loop construction.

(Below left) Oak flooring installed in opposing directions for a visual break; (right top) large, patterned area rug with fringe, and (bottom) rich, plush carpet.

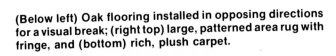

The clerestory lights up the windowless kitchen behind the fireplace and also floods light out into the living area.

(Above) The delicately-printed wallcovering and lacy chair give a special charm to this bathroom. (Below) A graceful archway between kitchen and dining room done in limestone design paneling. (Bottom) Platform and wall sections of simulated brick add a unique touch to a bedroom.

Folding doors (above) serve well for a spacious closet. (Below) A structural roof deck which plunges down over a tiled, indoor garden.

An ideal bathroom like the one above features large mirrors, ample counter space and plenty of drawers and cabinets. (Right) A handsomely color-contrasted whirlpool bath.

(Left) Traditional-style cabinets, fixtures and wallcovering give an antique touch to this bathroom. (Above) With a modular-unit bathroom vanity, extra glass shelves may be added for purely decorative purposes.

Four model living areas: (below top) a tasteful, contemporary-style dining nook in a split-level home; (bottom) a kitchen with warm, old-fashioned furniture; (top right) a hobby room/den with loom and weaving materials; (lower right) and a bath with wall-to-wall mirror and valance lighting.

(Top left) Peaceful dining with a picture window view. The bathroom (bottom left) has a warm whimsical quality. (Below top) unusual wrought-iron furniture and a paneled wall covered with old-fashioned sepia-tone photographs. And (below bottom) a versatile roof window.

A variety of features for the kitchen: (left) contemporary-style built-in cabinetry; (below top left) a ceiling light box over an eating and cooking island; (top right) the common over-the-sink window provides a good source of direct light during the day; (lower left) a flat surface built-in cook-top for easy cleaning; and (lower right) an island center with both work and eating facilities illuminated by a skylight.

A loft-type ceiling spanning two floors together with an absence of walls creates a feeling of immense space. Living areas are defined largely by floor coverings.

(Right) Living room with cathedral ceiling and windows. (Below) A three-level plan with living room and adjoining music room on the lower level.

(Above left) The two-story living room often found in a multilevel plan features a loft which can be used as a den or guest room. (Right) Another loft-like arrangement with sliding glass doors opening directly to the outdoors. (Below) Plants, lighting and unusual shaped windows in sky studio add drama to this arrangement.

(Right) Two levels of a four-level plan: contemporary-design living room with dining room above. The upholstery pattern is carried through from one level to the other. (Below) A galley-type kitchen featuring a double oven and wood-finish cabinets.

(Above) Although reversed, a similar split-level dining room/living room arrangement as seen on the opposite page. Again, the style of decor in both rooms is consistent. (Below) The outdoors is definitely indoors here. Natural light enters at right and through sliding glass door.

# WHAT ABOUT furniture

The choice of furniture style is important because it's the furniture, to a great extent, that determines the degree of formality or informality of your decorating scheme and what types of fabrics and other accessories you'll need.

The furniture you select should match your life style. So what shall it be: the classic elegance of formal French furniture? The warmth of Provincial? An eclectic mix? A '70s Modern? Thanks to modern manufacturing techniques, it's possible to have furniture of any period that will match your preference. Not too long ago, there were very definite rules about what colors and what architecture went with what period. Happily, the last few years have seen many changes in decorating, so you can break every rule and still create a successful environment for you and yours. Just take your pick of styles, here, to suit your life.

While a single style repeated throughout a small house is often appealing, there's no reason why you can't use different styles if you've more than one favorite. Where the main living area is an open floor plan—which usually means that the entry hall, living room, and dining room are inseparable—of course you should use either the same or compatible styles. A change of pace can be introduced in the other rooms.

Popularity of furniture styles has always run in cycles, their designs and general attributes affected by decorating trends. Rome, the Near East, and the Orient developed furniture which indirectly affected later designers, but scant attention is given here to styles prior to the 16th century, since they have had minor influence on today's furniture. In fact, the first significant major period, the Gothic, prevailed from 1100 to 1500 A.D. Massive and ornate, designed by churchmen and produced principally in monasteries, the furniture of this era was similar in all parts of Europe.

The 16th century witnessed the flowering of the Rennaissance—the revival of classical culture. The arts prospered. Furniture and cabinetmaking became honored crafts. Because of its classical origin, all Renaissance furniture has common characteristics, regardless of country of origin. Following this era, the demand for furniture began to grow and individual craftsmen began developing styles with national characteristics keyed to people's preferences.

Today's furniture descends directly from the great styles of the 17th and 18th centuries. Contemporary designers have borrowed from these traditional styles —improved on them, increased their comfort, and scaled them to modern homes. Mass production has brought well-designed furniture within the reach of all.

In common practice, the terms "period," "style," even "period style," are used interchangeably. Because we are dealing here with identification of design characteristics, "style" is used wherever applicable. A style relates to design characteristics identifying the work of a famous designer or school of designers. A period is a measure of historical duration.

In some cases (William & Mary), style and period coincide. In others (Georgian), the period includes several styles (Adam, Hepplewhite, and Chippen-

**This unquestionably unique sunken living room features built-in couches, stone fireplace and "cave drawing" wallcovering.**

dale). In still others (Gothic and Renaissance), styles were common to many countries and extended through several historical periods.

For most practical purposes, furniture can be divided into three *broad* classifications—traditional or classic, provincial or rustic, and contemporary, which is often referred to as modern. Let's take a closer look at these three classifications.

## Traditional Furniture

Traditional furniture includes the classic designs that are still being used today. Genuine antiques of the great furniture periods are so rare as to be out of the question for most families, but the continual advancement of technology has made it possible for almost anyone to own reproductions. The price range of reproductions runs the gamut from low to high, depending upon the intricacy of the original design and the quality that goes into its manufacture. Even with the highly advanced machinery available in modern furniture factories, it is still more costly to produce a traditional curved and carved Queen Anne chair leg than it is to turn out a straight and simple contemporary leg. A traditional chair, then will usually cost somewhat more than a contemporary chair of comparable size and quality.

Most styles were created for, and named in honor

of, the reigning monarchs of the period, for art and culture centered around the courts. Thus, we have Queen Anne, Jacobean (King James I), and Louis XIV, XV, and XVI. A student of history will note the relationship between the personality of the ruler and the character of the furniture. Later, especially in the Georgian period, the cabinetmaker came in for his fair share of credit. Chippendale, Adam, Sheraton, and Hepplewhite are some of the popular styles named for their creators.

When you look for traditional furniture in stores, or leaf through current home furnishings magazines, these are the periods you will see most often:

**William & Mary** (English, late 17th to early 18th century). In 1688, Mary, daughter of James II, and her husband, Prince William of Orange, accepted the throne of England, bringing with them from Holland numerous craftsmen and quantities of baroque furniture. During their reign, a style of furnishings emerged which was to be a transition between the elaborate forms of the Stuart period and the grace of the Queen Anne style. Pieces distinctive of the period were china cabinets, round and oval gate-leg tables, banister-back chairs with crestings, higher bedsteads (some reached 16 feet), small tables for gaming, and the newly developed chest-on-frame (highboy) and dressing table (lowboy). Walnut was the most popular wood during this era. Prominent characteristics of

**A Queen Anne writing table with scallopshell carved ornament.**

**A blend of styles: period chairs surrounding a contemporary table with iron grille work.**

William & Mary furniture include turnings in the shape of the inverted cut, the trumpet, gadrooning, perpendicular legs, the bun foot, the straight bracket foot, and the Spanish foot, with shaped stretchers often set crosswise between the legs.

**Queen Anne** (English, early to mid-18th century). Queen Anne, second daughter of James II, ruled England from 1702 until 1714. The furniture style that bears her name, however, covers a period of forty years and includes the reign of George I and part of the reign of George II. The style developed during this age of flourishing craftsmanship is considered one of the most graceful of the century. Its most distinctive feature is an undulating line based on the "S," or cyma, curve—an unbroken line with both a convex and concave curve. William Hogarth, the celebrated 18th-century English painter and engraver, called this curve the "line of beauty." The most fashionable wood was walnut, but mahogany was introduced about 1720. With the use of this wood, furniture became lighter and more graceful; and elaborate carving, to which mahogany was especially suited, began to appear. The Queen Anne chair is perhaps the most familiar design of the period. It has an extremely comfortable splat, often shaped to fit the back. Card tables with turnover hinged tops, small tables, and lower chests of drawers were popular. Queen Anne is also notable for the introduction of the ball-and-claw foot and the scallopshell carved ornament. Familiar reproductions today are the Queen Anne highboy with curved leg and scallopshell-adorned drawer fronts, pie-crust tables with tilting tops, and dining side chairs with slightly curved slat backs. The Queen Anne style is especially important, as you will learn later in this discussion, for its influence on the currently more popular American Colonial furniture.

**Chippendale** (English, mid-18th to early 19th century). Thomas Chippendale, the best-known and best-advertised figure in the history of furniture making, was born about 1718 and died in 1779. The first cabinetmaker to have his name associated with a furniture style, Chippendale was paradoxically a master of the derivative. Rarely inventive, he borrowed elements from Gothic, Chinese, and French designs and translated them into a new style. Walnut and fruitwoods, as well as mahogany, were widely used in America at this time, while English cabinetmakers preferred mahogany, an excellent wood for the crisp carving associated with Chippendale. Other popular Chippendale motifs included rococo or asymmetrical designs, simulated Chinese bamboo, the "C" scroll, and extensive use of fretwork. In scale, his furniture

has a graceful look agreeable to modern tastes. Secretaries and highboys ornamented by pediments at the top, pie-crust tables, camel-back sofas, and dining chairs with comfortably wide seats prevail.

In 1754 Chippendale published *The Gentlemen and Cabinet-Maker's Director*, and this established him in the public mind as one of the foremost furniture designers of the period. This publication is known to have reached America, and the style it delineated was adapted by American cabinetmakers to suit colonial tastes. For example, while the highboy or chest-on-frame went out of style in most parts of England in the mid-18th century, it continued in America and was developed in the American Chippendale style to include the elegant Philadelphia chest-on-chest, the Boston bombe-type chest-on-chest, and the handsome Newport block-front form. When we refer to "Chippendale" in this text, we are using the term in the American sense.

**Adam** (English, mid-18th to early 19th century). Architects as well as furniture designers, the two Adam brothers are known for the classic architectural details they added to cabinets—egg-and-dart moldings, wreaths, acanthus leaves—and their use of architec-

**A period dining-room set in rich walnut.**

tural columns as part of the construction of cabinets. They were much influenced by the excavation of Pompeii, which began in their time and led to a classical revival. They favored rectangular lines, relieved by round or tapered legs, bombe fronts on consoles, and hexagonal, octagonal, or oval designs on chair backs. Furniture in the Adam style was generally made of mahogany or satinwood, and cane-back pieces were popular.

**Hepplewhite** (English, mid-18th to early 19th century). Arm and side chairs with upholstered seats, and lyre, shield, or oval backs are synonymous with the Hepplewhite period. In storage pieces, there was a shift of emphasis to chests of drawers rather than the highboys and lowboys of Chippendale and Queen Anne. Legs were square and slightly tapered. For decoration, which he used sparingly, George Hepplewhite chose rosettes, medallions, and tasteful brass hardware.

**Sheraton** (English, mid-18th to early 19th century). The furniture of Thomas Sheraton needed only a small amount of carving and other embellishment, for its beauty was inherent in a delicate grace of line and the use of inlays that revealed the true loveliness of fine cabinet woods. His furniture is recognizable for

slender, graceful proportions that belie its strength and durability. The lightly sealed look of Sheraton— long, tapered legs; gently swelling fronts on consoles and sideboards; kidney-shaped desks; and caned settees—is appropriate in many contemporary homes.

**Victorian** (English, mid-19th to turn of the century). Named for Queen Victoria, who reigned for sixty-four years, from 1837 to 1901, the Victorian style prevailed in the United States for fifty years. Then enthusiastically accepted, it is now derogatorily referred to by most as the "Black Walnut and Horsehair Period." At present, some of the furniture may seem grotesque, if not merely ugly, but this period is one which no one interested in furniture can ignore. Briefly, an effort to machine process furniture (as a result of the Industrial Revolution), combined with little regard for aesthetic discernment (as a result of an intense— but indiscriminate—revival in numerous classic styles, especially Gothic), resulted in mass-produced, heterogeneously designed furniture. Although a severe indictment of the entire Victorian period, some more formal types have proven worthy of reproduction and have an inherent appeal difficult to find in any other period.

The Victorian era was one of sentimentality, primness, stodgy respectability, and all of these characteristics are vividly reflected in the furniture of the time. Developed primarily from Greek, Gothic, Louis XIV, and Elizabethan styles, Victorian furniture was heavy, formal, and substantially built. It may then easily be said that most of the furniture was not designed in the normal sense of the word, but assembled from old pieces of carving. Black walnut and rosewood were favored woods. Inlays of brass, wood, and mother-of-pearl were also extensively used. Favorite motifs are scrolls, foliage, pendants, bunches of grapes, and numerous nautical emblems. Seating pieces were generally upholstered: the most common fabrics were plush, haircloth, and tapestries; and trimmings were an abundance of needlework, fringes, braids, and tassels.

Among the more popular pieces of the era were sofas and love seats, as well as graceful oval-backed side chairs upholstered in velvet, needlepoint, or brocade, and adorned with such sentimental carvings as roses or grape clusters. Genuine examples of this period can often be identified by their decorative details, which were sometimes imported or carved elsewhere in the United States, and from a wood different from that of the main body of the chair.

Those seeking comfort in kitchens were turning to bentpost Victorian ladder-backed chairs, adorned with incised designs, or high-backed chairs deriving their interest from slender, closely spaced spindles. Rockers were often found in similar construction, with low-relief carving. In storage pieces, usually rectangular and large in scale, and in tables, usually more baroque, carved elements were frequently imposed upon the basic design. Bevel-edged marble tops and distinctive hardware, such as wooden drawer pulls carved to represent acorns and oak leaves, or brass pulls with intricately wrought back plates, were also trademarks. Although derived from Britain's Victoria Regina, examples of Victorian furniture commonly seen in this country were free American adaptations.

**Louis XIV** (French, mid-17th to early 18th century). A powerful monarch who reveled in luxurious, expensive living, Louis XIV inspired an ornate school of furniture design. Sofas and chairs were amply proportioned, endowed with curved arms and legs, lavishly carved, and enriched by tapestry, velvet, or damask upholstery. Inlays of ivory, mother-of-pearl, brass, and porcelain were popular.

**Louis XV** (French, early through mid-18th century). In contrast to the somewhat larger and heavier proportions of Louis XIV furniture, the Louis XV period is characterized by a delicacy that is distinctly feminine—a dead giveaway to the fact that certain lovely courtesans, notably Madame de Pompadour and Madame du Barry, were the powers behind the throne. Charming are the little writing desks, chaise longues, and occasional tables created at this time. Chairs had roomy seats to accommodate the ladies' voluminous skirts. Curved arms and legs and swelling cabinet fronts were the rule. Pieces were rich with ornamentation; and while some classic motifs were retained—wreaths, acanthus leaves, and the like—the baroque influence prevailed in complex carved embellishments.

**Louis XVI** (French, late 18th century). In France as well as England, the excavations of Pompeii brought about a return to classicism. Also at work was the revival of a democratic spirit and a distaste for the excesses of the aristocracy. As a welcome relief from the lavishness of Louis XV, furniture became more restrained, with straight lines replacing curves, and the familiar Roman and Greek motifs restored.

**Directoire** (French, late 18th century). At last, the people triumphed over the monarchy and France became a republic, ruled by a *Directoire* or triumvirate of men. In design, there was a striving to imitate the pure classicism of the ancient Greeks, whose government inspired the French Revolution. Furniture was broad, utilizing both straight and curved lines, and featured either square, tapered, or curved legs. Lozenges, brass arrows, stars, swags, and eagles were some of the motifs.

**These chairs and table have typical Queen Anne style cabriole legs.**

46

**Empire** (French, early 19th century). Napoleon
soon overthrew the Directoire, became emperor, and
saw to it that his influence prevailed even in the arts.
The new style of the Napoleonic Empire was heavy
in scale, military in feeling, and had a classic dignity
to its straight lines. Square legs, claw feet, and heavy
bases are characteristic. Important were the faithfully
copied motifs of Greece, Rome, and Egypt, the last
also symbolizing Napoleon's military victories in that
country. In addition to acanthus leaves, scrolls, hon-
eysuckle, and other familiar ornaments, Napoleon's
egoism and pride in battle were carved into or inlaid
in brass on Empire furniture—his initial "N" encircled
by a laurel wreath, eagles, torches, lions' heads, and
military trophies.

**Duncan Phyfe** (American, late 18th to mid-19th
century). One of the only American cabinetmakers to
achieve widespread and lasting fame, Phyfe borrowed from the Directoire and French Empire periods, for the sympathies of the Americans were with
the French rather than the English. Adding his own innovations, he eventually created the style known as
American Empire—as heavy as the French Empire, but
minus much of the decoration. The Duncan Phyfe
sofa had curved ends, flared legs, and claw or lion's-
paw feet. Although his creation of an American period has historic significance, he is more admired by
current standards for his earlier work, inspired by
Sheraton and Hepplewhite. These designs were slender and graceful, lending themselves to refined backgrounds. Best known are his lyre-backed chairs and
pedestal tables with tripods of flared legs.

**Federal** (American, late 18th to mid-19th century).
The Federal period is commonly divided into two periods: the Federal, extending from 1790 to 1825, and
American Empire, 1825 to 1830. With Duncan Phyfe—
the prophet of this period—setting the pace for other
craftsmen, the chief inspirations were French Empire
styles intermingled with 18th-century and Colonial
influences. Although based primarily upon the Sheraton style, American pieces of 18th-century inspiration are more severe than their English counterparts.
American pieces of Empire derivation are sturdier
and heavier than their French originals. Only the
simplest turnings are used, and American pieces are
frequently braced with stretchers. Where carving was
employed, the favorite motifs, typifying independ-
ence, were stars and eagles. Additional motifs were
acanthus, cornucopias, scrolls, and pineapples. Metal
mounts and glass knobs are used extensively. Sofas
have rolled arms. Chests have irregular fronts and
mirrors. Center tables rest on heavy pedestals. Sideboards are heavy and decorated with columns. Legs
of chairs, tables, and settees are straight. Reeded columns, claw feet, and bracket feet are commonly used.
Mahogany is the favored wood, with occasional use
of native oak, ash, hickory, and fruitwoods.

## Provincial or Rustic Furniture

Many people have a feeling of nostalgia for furniture of the past and a preference for the luxuriousness
of its soft lines, carving, and other embellishments.
On the other hand, they enjoy an informal, casual
type of living more suited to contemporary furniture
styles. For these persons, any of the Provincial styles
offers a good compromise.

Provincial furniture, as the name suggests, had its
origins in the outlying provinces that surrounded the
royal courts of London, Paris, and other sophisticated
European cities. All over the countryside, local carpenters and cabinetmakers would look to the cities
for design inspiration. What was fit for a king, of
course, was hardly suitable for life in a country cottage. Most of the people could not afford exact copies
of court furniture, nor did their cabinetmakers have
the skills nor materials necessary to reproduce them.
The resulting adaptations—ranging from the crudest
imitations to versions that were almost an improvement on the originals—have given us a rich heritage
of design admirably suited to our modern way of living.

In general, Provincial furniture imitated traditional
forms, but simplified them and eliminated the more
complex carving, inlays, and embellishments. Sometimes the scale was smaller to suit more modest
homes. In place of the fine, rare woods and rich fabrics that went into traditional furniture, materials
readily and inexpensively available locally were substituted. These are some of the currently popular Provincial furniture styles:

**Early American** (17th century). The hardships endured by the early settlers are familiar to everyone.
Mere survival was a full-time job for the entire family,
and luxuries were almost unknown for many years.
With what time and materials they could manage, the
men of the family made crude and simple furniture
for their roughhewn homes—oak or pine chests, ladder-backed chairs and rockers with rush seats, open
hutches, and harvest-style dining tables. In fact, not
until the emergence of American Jacobean furniture
in the 17th century do we have any record of a dominant style in colonial America. These massive Jacobean designs, made of oak, reflected the Elizabethan
ancestry of the Pilgrim carvers and joiners. Such features as bulbous supports, scrolls, strapwork, melon

turnings, fluting, and geometric carving were commonplace. The open-court cupboard and the press cupboard became household essentials; so did the oaktester beds, and rectangular table with stretchers and baluster legs. The earliest slat-backed chairs emerged—later to be refined as elegant Chippendale ladder-back designs. With the restoration of the monarchy under William and Mary, dramatic style changes occurred. Oak was replaced by walnut; furniture became lighter, more decorative. The first highboy is seen in the William & Mary high chest, featuring the first use of cyma or ogee curves. A better standard of living encouraged the design of new tables—porringer, tavern, splay-leg, and gateleg. Spiral turnings, serpentine stretchers, bun feet, rich upholstery, and crown crest motifs on chair tops were the newer, more formally decorative details; and there were new forms as well, like the daybed and the wing chair.

What most people think of as "Early American" originated with the maple furniture that was made in New England starting in the mid-17th century, and used for the less formal rooms of the house; they were Jacobean and William & Mary forms simplified. The gateleg table was restyled as the butterfly table. Slat-backed chairs were reinterpreted in maple, relieved of their bulbous decoration, often fitted with rockers. Developed somewhat later were the maple cupboards, cabinets, and the superb spindle chairs of the Windsor group—low back, comb back, hoop back, New England arm, fan back, and loop back. Folklore claims the popular Windsor was born when George II discovered it in a peasant's cottage, and was impressed with its rare comfort and simplicity. The ancestry of some of today's Early American cabinets can be traced back to curly maple chest-on-chests and slant-top desks with bracketed straight feet. But what is commonly referred to as Early American is really a combination of authentic designs and country reinterpretations—which evolved much later—of cabinets, beds and tables in simple maple expressions.

**American Colonial** (18th century). While Early American maple furniture was slender and light in scale, the pine furniture that began to show up early in the 18th century was heavier, bolder, more imposing—emulating many features of American Jacobean designs. In our museums we see examples of New England pine cupboards with fielded panels and cyma-scrolled framework. Separate corner cabinets, which came in during the William & Mary period, were especially popular in the South, while pine dressers, topped with open shelves, were familiar in kitchens all along the American coast. The Southern

china press, made with arched panel doors, is another example of the prototypic pine designs which have endured. So is the Pennsylvania German (Dutch) pine cupboard of the early 18th century in which a combination of woods was often employed. We have seen pine tavern tables with maple tops, and the New England hutch table—a humble relative of the chair table—also made of pine and maple. And a far cry from the massive William & Mary designs were the remarkably graceful Queen Anne styles, developed during the first quarter of the 18th century. Side chairs with undulating splats, and the cabriole leg, with its dramatically curving knee, dominated furniture design for most of the century. Broken scroll pediments on case pieces and shell ornamentation on highboys and chair backs were best known and cherished

**American Colonial cupboard and Windsor-style chairs.**

Queen Anne "leit motifs." Named after the great English cabinetmaker who inspired it, the Chippendale style appeared later in the century, supplanting the Queen Anne cabrioles with its straight legs, introducing pierced splat and pretzel ladder-backed chairs, and innovating new forms such as Pembroke tables, bookcases, block-front chests, and serpentine-back sofas.

**Late 18th-or Early 19th-Century American.** The classic period of American furniture design falls between the years 1790 and 1830, and includes a variety of influences—Adam, Hepplewhite, and Sheraton, the renowned English cabinetmakers of the period. Adam's fascination with the Renaissance architects comes through in such contributions as tapering furniture legs, which were turned, fluted, and reeded, as well as pilasters and light moldings, emphasizing structural lines. Hepplewhite styled his shield, heart-shaped and oval-backed chairs, while Sheraton stressed reeded posts for beds and classical, elegant armchairs. Federal craftsmen looked beyond England to the continent, but purely American concepts, such as the eagle and shield of Duncan Phyfe of New York marked America's new pride. Today's versions of this period are highly simplified, but we can trace cross-banding, multipedestal tables, and decorative molding to this era.

In the middle of this century, some designer coined the phrase, "form follows function." Yet the Shakers, an American religious sect deriving from the Quakers, had said it first, a hundred years earlier, in the simple credo of their furniture design. All articles of their furniture were to be devoid of embellishment; the style of the furniture was, quite simply, its structure. The most interesting Shaker contributions were built-in cupboards and dressers, chairs and rockers—painted or stained but never lacquered—and cot-like beds on rollers, a concept that survives today. Finials "grew" out of chair posts and were not an after-thought; seats were rush, splint, plaited straw, or leather. Natural wood grain was emphasized, and Shakers excelled at basketmaking.

Stenciled or hand-decorated furniture encompasses every period of American furniture design. From Jacobean to Victorian, craftsmen popularized this inexpensive way to embellish and protect furniture. The styles that survive today trace their ancestry to the Pennsylvania German (Dutch) designs and the stenciled Hitchcock chairs and Salem rockers of Connecticut and Massachusetts. Typical German designs were scroll-backed chairs, dower chests, and wardrobes painted with favored motifs—tulips, birds, fruit, unicorns, geometric stars—Rhineland folk art. Hitchcock chairs, stenciled with gilt, and the colorful Windsor rockers of Salem, raised stenciling to a fine art in America. Actually, Windsor chairs were originally made by wheelwrights rather than cabinetmakers, hence the use of a bentwood back frame, supported by spindles, and legs pegged into saddle seats. Many variations in shape, such as comb, fan, hoop, and bow backs, rockers and braced backs, were common. Some models were given the names of the city of origin or of prominent users. Later, settees, beds, tables, and other pieces were introduced. Woods were varied: pine and birch for the seats; hickory, ash, and birch for the bent parts; and oak, maple, and birch for

**A kitchen with a distinctively American Colonial flavor.**

turned parts.

**French Provincial.** While the best of French period furniture is lovely, with its graceful curves, fine carving, and exquisite use of delicate fabrics, most modern families would find it a bit too ornate and impractical for their mode of living. The availability of French Provincial therefore, is indeed a blessing. A restrained adaptation of Louis XV and other styles, French Provincial makes good use of the curved leg, bombe front, painted finishes, and somewhat feminine characteristics of the originals. Decoration, however, is much simplified.

Early French Provincial style was confined largely to functional pieces, such as bunk beds, stools, benches, commodes, wardrobes and trestle tables. The 18th-century pieces (those principally reproduced today) offer a wide variety of styles in chairs, tables, desks, buffets, chests, wardrobes, and clocks. Local cabinetmakers produced comfortable, unpretentious pieces simply decorated, that maintain a remarkably continuing popularity. But as furniture became more available, certain traits native to the provinces became more discernible. Ladder-backed chairs were developed in Normandy and Burgundy. Ladder-backed settees were made in Provence. Straw-seated chairs were common in Poitou, Vendee, and other provinces. Solid top-rails were characteristic of Breton workmen. Chairs have flat, curved arms, resting on turned supports; and legs are either straight or cabriole—sometimes upholstered, sometimes ending in bun feet. Stretchers, some straight, some turned, some curved, appear on chairs and many other pieces.

Armoires (linen cabinets) were common to all provinces and were given a place of honor in the home. Beds have high posts and canopies, usually with enclosed draperies. (In Breton, the *lit closee*—or closed bed—resembled a huge cupboard with its solid wood-paneled sides, and afforded a certain degree of privacy as well as protected against the cold, damp drafts of that area.) Tables, chests, and cupboards often have shaped aprons. Many chests and buffets have curved fronts. Early tables were of the trestle type but later ones have cabriole legs. Upholstered pieces followed the general design of the court furniture they copied; but decoration was simplified. Moldings were the favorite form of decoration. Paneling and carving in geometric and conventional designs replaced the inlay of the court pieces. Depth of carving varied, but was generally deep in Burgundy, and shallow in Provence. Brass, copper, and steel hardware predominated. Large locks, oversized

hinges, and key plates served as decorative details. Native woods such as walnut, beech, wild cherry, elm, and oak were widely employed.

**Italian Provincial.** Early Italian Provincial furniture shows the strong influence of the Italian baroque style; even though the local craftsmen eliminated the lavish decoration, they maintained a general exaggeration of scale and line and color. Late Italian Provincial is of neoclassical inspiration and was strongly influenced by the French styles of the late 18th and 19th centuries. This later style is the one most commonly designated and accepted today as Italian Provincial, since the designs have been scaled down and reproportioned. Only the most graceful pieces have been

**Chest and mirror in the French Provincial style.**

revived. Lines of cabinets, sideboards, desks, and chests are predominantly rectangular, with straight, square, tapered legs. Where curves appear in tables and dining chairs and occasional pieces, they are smooth, graceful, and unbroken by ornament. Brass hardware is common, and molding often follows the outline of drawer or door. Woods used were walnut, olive, and fruitwoods; mahogany, probably for economic reasons, was seldom used. Surfaces were sometimes painted or enameled.

**Mediterranean.** Two countries on the north shore of the Mediterranean Sea—Spain and Italy—contributed greatly to European furniture styling in the 16th and 17th centuries (so-called Italian and Spanish Renaissance periods), when local craftsmen, using native woods and materials, built furniture for local use. Most evident in this developing style was the influence of the Moors, who loved geometric design, bright colors, and metal work, which the Spanish and Italian artisans adopted. This Mediterranean furniture ranged from nearly primitively functional to extremely formal, with Spanish interpretations favoring the vigorous, masculine look with deep moldings, while Italian versions are more restrained. For centuries, it has retained a constant appeal in certain areas, but only recently has it enjoyed widespread popularity in this country under the designation of Mediterranean furniture.

The intrinsic charm of Mediterranean furniture is in its simplicity, its boldness of design, and its vigorous lines. Pieces are "built to the floor" with comparatively short, squat, ornately turned legs and feet. Facades of chests, cupboards, cabinets, and bed headboards have a sculptural feeling, with decorations of frets and guilloches. Hardware is heavy, sometimes burnished. Hip-joint chairs have frames suggesting two semi-circles joined together; one set forms the legs, the other the framework of the seat. Geometric interlacing, turned spindles, and metal grille work are common. Ornamental wrought-iron underbraces for tables and chairs often appear. Walnut is the most fashionable wood, followed by oak, pine, chestnut, and fruitwoods.

Architectural elements in a room enhance the appeal of Mediterranean design—paneled doors, beamed ceilings, and dark-stained woodwork. Perhaps more than any other of the styles now in popular usage, Mediterranean is more a look than a type of furniture. All elements must blend to create a harmonious whole. Stucco-textured white walls; decorative wrought iron used in grilles and brackets and in such accessories as candelabras and lamps; and the beautiful tiling of the Old World—all these combine with the trestle tables with their curved supports, and high-backed chairs with their intricately turned stretchers—to create a distinctive atmosphere.

**Contemporary Furniture**

Almost everyone is able to recognize contemporary design, where the emphasis is on function rather than frills. According to the theory of the modernists, beauty is inherent in the shape of an object and the materials that go into it, making added embellishments superfluous.

Until the time of the 1935 Paris Exposition, almost all American furniture consisted of reproductions of historical periods. Inspired by the *"art moderne"* style of the French, American designers turned their attention to the creation of truly modern furniture. These early designers relied on geometric forms and exotic woods. They were greeted with some wonder and much ridicule, but they did pave the way for today's modern furniture. Following these early efforts, progress was rapid. The famous design school, Bauhaus of Germany, made outstanding contributions to modern furniture design. More and more American designers, like Gilbert Rohde, created pieces of simple design, practical utility, and wide public appeal. The Chicago Exposition of 1933 gave modern furniture further impetus. Today it is by far the most popular single style.

In considering contemporary or modern furniture, however, it should be remembered that modern can't be defined and delineated as historical periods are. Styles such as Victorian, Louis XIV, and Chippendale have firmly established characteristics, common lines, ornamental and decorative details. Types of legs, arms, backs, and pediments, and similar identifying features are historically fixed. Modern, on the other hand, is a style still developing, and it promises to remain in a state of transition for many years to come. New changes occur as contemporary designers add their interpretations, ranging from simplification and adaptation of traditional designs to original creations bordering on the bizarre.

Several different types of modern have appeared. Some have already been discarded, such as the "waterfall front" commerical styles of the 1930s, and the angular, geometric forms of the late 1920s. Others, like the pre-World War II "Classical Modern" and "Swedish Modern," based on updating of classic forms, have had an influence on contemporary and future modern furniture.

The Scandinavians are recognized as the masters of

the contemporary; they brought a softened, sculptured look to the clean-lined simplicity of contemporary design forms. Oiled walnut and teak are their favorite woods. Scandinavian designers are famous for perfecting chairs molded to fit the contours of the body. They were also leaders in the recent innovation of suspending almost everything but beds and chairs from the wall in order to save space and eliminate the clutter of legs.

The Japanese have made their influence felt in contemporary Oriental design, the characteristics of which are extremely low tables, large pillows for lounging on the floor, red and black lacquer finishes, and the use of *shoji* screens as room dividers. The idea is to achieve serenity by keeping furnishings to a minimum.

So-called "Oriental" furniture is a blend of styles from different countries. Furniture with an Oriental label, like modern, is crisp and straight-lined, and often lacquered in brilliant colors. Modern enthusiasts favor Oriental because of its ability to make small spaces seem larger. The young and the not-so-young like it for its combination of practical, yet exotic qualities.

In any consideration of current modern or contemporary furniture, the mass production methods of present factories must be carefully considered. Clean, simple lines and the elimination of unnecessary ornamentation have made modern furniture quite practical for quantity production. As long as this condition prevails, and as long as American tastes lean toward the restrained, unembellished forms, modern will enjoy maximum popularity.

The furniture mentioned thus far is constructed of wood. A suitable furniture wood is strong and hard enough to withstand use, but not so hard that it is difficult or expensive to work with. It should take glue easily, be free of imperfection, and be properly kiln-dried to minimize defects such as shrinking, swelling, warping, the splitting of uneven joints, and checking. Woods best adapted to different parts and to construction processes should be used. It's often difficult, however, to judge the quality of wood. For example, the quality of the drying is as important in any piece of furniture that you buy as are its looks. Unfortunately, this is hard for you to determine for yourself when viewing a newly made piece of furniture. The best guarantee is a reputable manufacturer, large or small. A large manufacturer with a good reputation will tend to guarantee quality because he alone can afford to have his own kilns and supervise them in such a way that the wood is put into production only when it is at

an optimum level of dryness. Aside from the manufacturer's reputation, you can protect yourself by looking carefully at the surface wood and any parts of the wood frame that may be exposed. See if there is any warpage or splitting, and check to see that the grain runs straight.

Other materials are frequently employed in manufacturing contemporary furniture. The most common are:

**Metal.** Metals have been used in furniture making since the early periods of the Egyptian and Chinese cultures. Later, the Medieval and Renaissance periods were rich in furniture made with metal parts, and it was found in use for structural details of Spanish, French, and Italian furniture from 1500 to 1700. But in the late 18th century there was a decrease in the splendor of metal in furniture. While there have been several attempts to revive it, metal furniture has had no great general acceptance among today's buyers.

Lack of warmth and texture are metal's greatest disadvantages. It does, however, blend well with other furniture materials—wood, plastic, and glass, for instance—to make it more interesting and attractive. Metal, of course, is very strong; will not crack or warp; is rather easy to shape and fabricate; and is light in weight, even lighter than wood. Permanent finishes can be baked on it.

One of the earliest, and still most popular of all the metal furniture forms, is that made of wrought iron. When properly designed, it is attractive, robust, and yet intricate. Wrought-iron bases are used in various Italian and Spanish furniture styles, while many pieces of oak furniture have finely ornamented wrought-

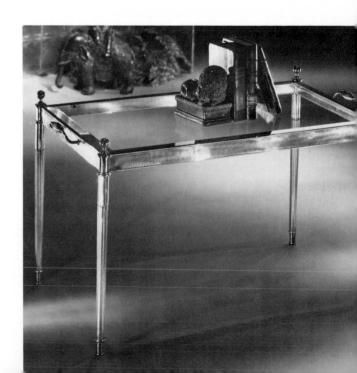

**A handsome metal and glass table.**

**Wicker and other similar furniture has become increasingly popular.**

iron pulls.

Contemporary wrought-iron furniture, which is generally combined with glass, tiles, plastic, or panel wood, is used on terraces, in play areas, and may be either rustic or urban in style.

Late in the 19th and early in the 20th century, cast iron and brass tubing found their way into furniture design. In fact, the brass bedstead, made of brass tubing, has recently made somewhat of a comeback with interior decorators and in some furniture collections.

In some contemporary furniture, various forms and types of steel, as well as aluminum, chromium, and magnesium, have proved to be practical and have had a fair degree of popularity. In most cases, the use of metal becomes an integral part of actual construction. Touched surfaces—seats, backs, and arms—are covered with, or made of, wood, raffia, leather, reed, fabric, or other materials. Chromium plating is the typical finish on steel tubing, while lacquer and other processes provide a wider range of permanent metal finishes.

**Cane, Rattan, Bamboo, Wicker, and Similar Materials.** Except for bamboo, these materials don't have great strength, and must depend upon a more rigid framework of wood or metal. Since furniture made of these materials has a light, cool look, it is frequently used for tropical effects or for summer purposes. Design is fairly limited; it is variously woven or bent into the desired shapes.

Rattan is an Asiatic vine which is used to produce cane and reed, as well as rattan. Actually, the latter is a hollow tube left after the reed cane has been used. Before application to the framework, the reed or rattan is treated by singeing, to remove all the outer skin's fibrous threads. Then it is soaked until it's pliable. Generally, reed and rattan are finished with either a light-colored or clear lacquer.

Cane is the outside casing of the rattan stem. Although some furniture is made of cane, it is usually cut lengthwise into pieces and used for the weaving of chair seats. Rush is a long, twisted and woven grass that is also used for seating. It is found in the provincial chairs of every country.

Wicker and willow are almost synonymous as far as furniture construction is concerned. These pliable withes, or branches, come from both the willow and cottonwood trees. Willow is a native wood which is adaptable to weaving. Fiber is a euphemistic title for twisted paper material made from wood pulp employed to imitate wicker, rush, or cane.

Bamboo has a great deal of strength despite its light weight, and can be worked into designs of great interest and beauty, providing the joinery techniques are adequately applied.

**Glass, Marble, and Leather.** Glass is a hard and cold-feeling material that has practical use in furniture construction, and is used primarily combined with other materials. For instance, glass table tops are popularly used on both wood and metal tables. But, since glass can be molded or bent, totally glass furniture is

**An attractive, contemporary dinette set.**

possible, and as our technology progresses, it may become practical and desirable.

Marble tops for tables and bureaus have long been in use. They have a luxury and durability beyond almost any other furniture construction material. Because of its weight, however, marble requires a strong framework to hold it.

Leather is an old-time furniture material. It was originally used as seating material and was suspended over the open space between the legs. It had the additional asset of flexibility and could be used for folding furniture. Later, it was used decoratively to cover the arms and legs as well as the seats of chairs. When deep upholstery of furniture became fashionable, leather was used extensively for large, comfortable chairs. Up until the 18th century, leather was used in heavy weights which predisposed it to solid and heavy designs. As the century progressed, reverse calf, suede, and glove leather came into use. They are thinner and more flexible, and can be used on lighter and more elegant designs, but they are also more fragile. Today, leather is widely used, especially in the more modern designs, as it seems to combine particularly well with metal, plastic, stone, and tile, which are all dear to contemporary designers.

This widespread usage has influenced more than seating. Leather has always been used for screens, chests and on walls and Spanish desk tops, and by the French for various table tops. Today, entire rooms, tables, lamps, and every conceivable surface are being covered with leather. There are even leather bedspreads.

**Plastics.** Plastics are becoming a popular contemporary furniture material. As presently manufactured, plastic materials shouldn't be considered a low-cost substitute for wood; but, rather, as materials that are used because of their own characteristics. As always, new materials bring many new designs. For instance, a four-legged wooden accessory table looks the way it does because it is built in accordance with the raw material. Made of plastic, it could have many legs or none; be a cone, a cube, a ball; or even a giant nut and bolt. These new plastic designs uniquely fit today's way of life because they are flexible, mobile, innovative, and easy to maintain.

The variety of plastics and production methods used today enable the manufacturer to bring the consumer a wide range of intricate styles and details which might otherwise be unavailable by so-called standard materials and methods of production. The

**A shelf arrangement of modern design and materials.**

durability of plastics also enables the consumer to select the desired styles without having to worry about long, hard use and abuse by children, or any of a dozen considerations previously involved in selecting home furnishings. Now consumers can get what they really want or choose what they can best utilize.

Modern furniture rarely has the carving and surface detail that traditional styles do, and the lack of surface detailing makes it an ideal choice for casual living and for people who want to whisk through housework. Also, in its many moods, modern can live easily with all tones of all colors. Decorating latitude is great; apart from choices in glass and chrome, pieces come in light or dark woods.

**Upholstered Furniture**

Upholstered furniture is often called the "royal family" of the living room because it gives the appearance of comfort and the deep-seated ease of the 20th-century living room. Upholstered sofas and chairs not only give comfort, but they also offer a pleasant feeling of solidity and color. In addition, of course, upholstered furniture generally has a lasting quality of style.

Because of their size and importance, upholstered pieces should be positioned first in your room decorative arrangement, not only to preserve the balance of the plan, but because the sofa is generally the center of the main conversation group. Too many upholstered pieces are as unpleasant as too few. It's also important to remember that often a sofa or chair that looks just right in the store will be out of place in your home because of size.

For a feeling of lightness in a small living room, it

56

would be wise to consider a sofa with exposed wood frame and cane back or arms. By exposed wood, we mean that the wood frame is left showing as a decorative addition to the design on a partially upholstered piece. It can have a natural or painted finish.

In a large room, a completely upholstered sofa is in far better scale. A completely upholstered piece has exposed casters, bare legs, a wood base; or, it can hide these under a fabric skirt. The latest trend is called total upholstery; it refers to pieces that are often very large and upholstered all over, including the arms, legs and feet. Even open-arm chairs are now being covered top to bottom in upholstery fabric without an inch of wood showing. By varying the scale of basic furniture shapes, you can often create a completely different mood for your room. If you like the warm look and comfort of a club chair or barrel chair but your room is too small, try using a scaled-down version. Scaled-down means, in many cases, a difference of only a few inches, but these inches will make all the difference in your room's over-all effect.

Variations of skirts and cushions for backs and seats can change the look of a basic furniture style. A loose back and seat, for example, mean that separate cushions are set in the seat and against the back; these are individual pillows and are upholstered on all sides. Tight back and seat refers to sofas or chairs with plain backs and seats without separate cushions. A luxurious effect is achieved with tufted or buttoned upholstery. Tufting is tying down sections of fabric with buttons, leaving a puffy area in between. Each area of fabric is folded, tacked down, and stuffed individually, allowing fullness and flexibility. Buttoning is a less expensive version of tufting. The button is placed on a plain upholstered surface and tacked to the inner upholstery, causing a tufted look, but without the extra fullness of good tufting. Pull-up or side chairs often have slip seats—the seat is separate and can be lifted out of the frame of the chair when it needs reupholstering. In quality furniture, you usually have cushion and skirt styles. A skirt—either kick-pleat or box-pleat—on a sofa or chair will add to the effect of bulk and size, yet maintains a lighter feeling. Attached cushions and a tight seat or back without cushions also make a piece of furniture look lighter and smaller. An important point to remember in buying a sofa is that no matter what style, the length must fit the size of your room. The most beautiful sofa, if it's too long or too short, can ruin the effect you're trying to create. Incidentally, nowadays the difference between a couch and a sofa is not clearly defined. Traditionally, however, a couch (from the French *coucher*—to lie down) refers to a piece that has only one arm and possibly a back, and is intended more as a daybed, to be reclined on rather than sat on; whereas a sofa is a more luxuriously upholstered piece, with two arms and a back.

Sofa and chair styles are dependent on details such as the type of arm or back, or the over-all shape. Often these characteristics are used interchangeably and are found in several styles. For instance, the *Lawson sofa*, which is extremely versatile for both traditional and modern use, is completely upholstered, with a low, square back and outward-turning, rolled arms, which are lower than the back, and the most obvious characteristic of this sofa.

Since the final selection of the style of upholstered chairs and sofa is totally up to you, it may be wise to make some mention of the fibers used in modern upholstered furniture. Actually, combining synthetics and natural fibers creates fabrics with higher tensile strength, stronger abrasive resistance, easier cleanability, and more decorative interest. Cotton, a fiber widely used in upholstery, can be given added style by blending it with acetate, rayon, or nylon. These fibers are sometimes used alone. Here is a guide to

**A totally new concept in form and upholstery.**

most commonly used synthetic fibers.

1. *Acetate* is the generic name for a man-made compound of cellulose. It can take an unlimited range of dyes. When woven with cotton, nylon, or rayon, acetate can take one color and the other fiber another for interesting decorative effects. (Cross-dyeing.)

2. *Nylon* is one of the most durable upholstery fibers, having high abrasion resistance and excellent cleanability. It may be used alone, or can be mixed with other fibers. Nylon fabrics can have a luxurious wool look.

3. *Olefin* (Polypropylene) is a fiber of extremely high abrasion resistance and strength. This fiber has outstanding resistance to staining and unusually good soil-release qualities, which guarantee easy cleanability.

4. *Rayon* is the oldest man-made fiber and the most widely used of the synthetics. It can be dyed any color and can have the look and appearance of fabrics ranging from silk to wool.

5. *Polyester* is the newest of the synthetic fibers and one of the most highly resistant to abrasion, stretching, and shrinking. It is easy to dye, and when used in a blend with cotton, prints beautifully and cleans easily.

The advent of stain-repellent finishes has increased the life-span of upholstered furniture by keeping surfaces relatively dirt- and spot-free. Most fabrics sold today are therefore finished with a stain-repellent coating. The best known are *Zepel*® by DuPont and 3M's *Scotchgard*®. Since these offer resistance to everyday soiling, most spills will sponge off easily.

### Built-ins

Built-ins give almost any room in a house a customized appearance. Used imaginatively and tastefully, built-ins can help create the look of livability.

Let's take a look at some of the more common built-in furniture and see how it can be employed.

**Bookcases.** We have never met a person who is turned off by books. It's psychological. Most people like to think they are well-informed. Therefore, built-in bookcases are a "safe" decorating technique.

Bookcases should be used in all shapes, sizes, co-

(Top) Built-in bookcases are ideal for a child's room. (Bottom) This combination cabinet and bookcase serves for storage and is also an asset to the decor.

58

lors, and designs, with painted, stained, varnished, polished, or rough woods. They are relatively easy and inexpensive to construct, plus they can hide a multitude of architectural sins. For instance, an odd-sized high window—a pain-in-the-neck area for most decorators—can be made attractive by building a self-contained desk and bookcase treatment around it. Or an odd-shaped wall can give warmth and special purpose by using a built-in floor-to-ceiling bookcase. But, in either case, don't load the bookcase to the hilt with volumes of hardcover books. Instead, use plants, accessories, and perhaps even a portable television set to give it some sort of wall-unit effect.

Imagination is important when designing built-in bookcases. For example, a bookcase backed with randomly spaced mirrored inserts that are visible between the books is an excellent stimulant for the imagination and adds a strong element of warmth.

For a family room, the bookcases can be filled with items that would normally be found only in a person's home—trophies, family photographs, party games, anything imaginable to give the home a lived-in feeling.

One thing to consider when including bookcases in a living room is size. Build them large, even massive. Most people usually prefer floor-to-ceiling bookcases, even if the ceiling is pitched. Another popular use of bookcases is to flank a fireplace.

**Headboards.** Built-in headboard treatments are another excellent decorating suggestion. It's also a good way to get away from the furniture-store look where every piece—headboard, nightstand, wardrobe, and dresser—matches.

Headboards in a master bedroom can consist of shelf-and-storage combinations; they serve the purpose of a night stand but avoid its space-consuming presence. To add a strong element of drama, use mirrors in a headboard treatment, and give a smaller bedroom the appearance of a master suite.

Children's bedrooms also are natural places to use built-ins, especially headboards. Several imaginative headboard treatments are shown in this book, and they're not that difficult to construct either. Of course, built-in toy boxes and window seats with storage areas are excellent for avoiding the traditional cluttered look found in practically every child's room. A built-in desk butted up against the wall with overhead bookshelves transforms a smaller bedroom into a children's learning room.

**Modular Built-in Storage Units.** One thing that every home can use is extra storage room. Thus, when

decorating, it would be a good idea to consider building some storage cabinets, shelves, and a variety of other units into the structure of the rooms of your house. Frank Lloyd Wright was a master of this, providing such planned storage throughout his handsome houses. Nooks, crannies, and other space under windows, in odd corners, in hallways, and everywhere else were carefully utilized for built-in storage. Wright's homes were, as a result, noted for their great, spacious, uncluttered interiors, and their limitless capacity to sop up and put out of sight every kind of household possession not in use.

While custom-made built-ins can be constructed by a craftsperson to fit specific needs, the so-called modular, factory-made storage component is a good substitute for the average person. These units—produced by most of the leading kitchen cabinet manufacturers—offer great flexibility, maximum effi-

**A room with a style all its own.**

ciency, proven design, and a cost saving. Because they are produced in large quantities, they are much less expensive than one-of-a-kind, custom-made units.

Modular wall design means, of course, that the size and intrinsic design of all parts and components of a series of products are based on a fundamental common-denominator dimension, or module. The classic simplicity of Japanese construction has long been governed by a module based on their centuries-old 3-by-6-foot floor mat. In much United States construction today, simplicity and reduced costs stem from the use of a module four inches wide. All other key dimensions are multiples of that module, and that adds up to great interchangeability of parts, and thus, great versatility. Most modular units are available in sizes from 12 to 48 inches wide.

Also available is modular wall storage furniture which is engineered so that cabinet units can be grouped together with the flexibility of building blocks. Sizes usually range from 24 inches to 48 inches in width. They offer several advantages: you can start with only a few units and add on as you want or as your needs require; and since they are not fastened to the walls like custom- and factory-built cabinetry, their locations can easily be switched if you change your decorating plans. However, modular storage furniture is bulkier than most custom-built units.

The possibilities of putting built-ins to work in your

**These built-in bunk beds save space as well as provide drawers for storing blankets or clothes.**

**Well-designed cabinet units are practical and attractive in a bathroom.**

home are endless—vanities, linen cabinets, and wardrobe units for baths, powder rooms, and dressing rooms; fine furniture-type hutches, bars, and special-purpose cabinetry for dining areas; book shelves, bar units, and special cabinetry for games and hobbies in family rooms; beautiful cabinetry to house televisions, stereos, and other equipment in recreation rooms; desks for dens; and bureaus 'for bedrooms. But when selecting modular units, remember that accessibility is all important. Locate new cabinets and other units as close as possible to where they will be used in the over-all living plan. Use your space sensibily and efficiently. No need to go hog-wild with new units, blanketing every wall with all the cabinets you can get. But do plan well and do look for little-used space in a room, hall, or any other such place, that can be neatly appropriated to satisfy your storage needs. Similarly, every storage unit you get need not be propped up against a wall. Use your imagination and you'll be amazed at other places that are suitable for free-standing or semi-free-standing units. Such units often can be utilized as room dividers or separators, thus serving an architectural function as well.

# WALLS, FLOORS, CEILINGS AND
# windows

# 4

The walls, floor, ceiling, and windows are the background of any room. As such, they contribute directly to the feeling you wish to create in the room. In other words, the background surfaces help create the atmosphere in which you want to live through the ornamentation you place on them or leave off.

Backgrounds are coming to the fore in decorating up-to-date rooms. There is a sound reason for this. Walls (including the doors and windows) may comprise more than two-thirds of a room. They are actually its largest and most noticeable feature. Everywhere you look, your eye is carried to and stopped by a wall. And when you add the floor and ceiling you have nothing left in the cube you call a room but space. Thus, these background areas are what makes a room a room—decoratively speaking.

In selecting the backgrounds for your rooms, however, bear in mind the end result you wish to achieve. Rough surfaces, in general, have the connotation of informality, while the use of smooth slick materials implies a greater elegance.

## WALLS

At the very outset you must decide whether the walls, according to the room location and use, are to be a decorative entity—as when you use, for example, the continuous panorama of a beautiful scenic wallpaper; or whether they're to be a foil—a subtly blending part of the background. As a rule, rooms that are little used, that is, rooms in which you stay for relatively short periods of time, such as the foyer, hall, or dining room, can take bolder wall treatments (if you

wish) than those rooms where you settle down for relaxation, conversation, and reading, as in the living room, library, or bedroom. Generally, walls become correspondingly bold in direct ratio to the lessening of other decorative background competition such as that in draperies, lively rugs, or many colorful pictures.

To get a total insight into the part your walls will play, some decorators suggest that you remove all the furniture from the room, leaving just the carpet or rug. The floor covering is left in the room because it's important in your wall planning scheme. That is, a wall color is usually selected to blend with or complement the carpet or rug. In an otherwise bare room, knowing your total decorating plan, you can easily determine the part your walls should play.

The most common wall decorating materials are paint, wallcoverings, paneling and planking.

### Paint

Paint can transform any room in your home far more quickly and inexpensively than any other material available. A new coat of paint on your walls can bring with it a sparkle and beauty that should delight every member of your household and make your furnishings seem twice as attractive as they now seem. And applied correctly, it may have to be renewed only at long intervals, depending on your own requirements and tastes.

Two major considerations for the home decorator when he or she is planning to decorate with paint are the selection of which color and type of paint are best

**Rough, textured walls are most effective when light in color.**

for the purpose. Since there are so many sources of information on color, only a few facts related to paint that are especially important will be given here.

In selecting colors from paint chips, remember that the color will be intensified and appear much darker on the wall than it does in the small sample. Colors intensify when used in large amounts. And whether the finish is dull or shiny is almost as important as the color. A dull finish gives walls soft tones for background, while a shiny high gloss reflects light and may cause a glare. For a detailed discussion on the effects of various colors on room size and feeling, see Chapter 2.

In redecorating walls, you must consider the ceiling as part of the project. For best light reflection in a room, the ceiling should be very light in color. A white or off-white is best. For a bedroom that is used only for sleeping and dressing, it's not necessary to be so careful about light reflection, but if the room is used for studying, reading, sewing, or other close work, light is very important. You may use the same color on the ceiling as on the walls; or add white to the wall color for a lighter ceiling; or add a little of the wall color to white, to make the two surfaces blend more closely. If the ceiling is extra high and you wish to make it appear lower, paint it a little darker than the wall, but this will also make your room seem a little darker, especially at night. Another solution to the extra high ceiling problem is to bring the ceiling color down on the upper wall to form a border. (If molding is installed at this level, it should be painted the same color as the wall.) This border might be 6 to 18 inches wide depending on the height of the ceiling. On the other hand, if you want to add height to a room with a low ceiling, paint the ceiling white.

One popular wall treatment of the 1960s that has lost favor with most decorators in recent years is the one-wall-emphasis technique. In it, one wall was usually painted a deeper tone value of the same color than the other three. This one-wall emphasis made a square room lose its boxlike appearance and overcame the handicap of too few wall accessories and too little furniture. Frequently, it brought an element of excitement into what might otherwise be an architecturally drab room. While the painted deeper tone is seldom seen today, the same effect is frequently achieved by using wallcovering; or paneling on one wall and paint or another kind of wallcovering on the other three.

Woodwork is a part of the room background. The trend today is to make it as inconspicuous as possible. (In many new houses woodwork around doors and

windows is completely eliminated.) It is usually more pleasing to keep the color of the woodwork as near that of the walls as possible, since door and window shapes often cut into the walls and don't always form pleasing divisions. If the walls are painted, use the same color of paint on the woodwork. This will help to unify the background and make a small room appear larger. Contrasting color in the woodwork calls attention to it and breaks the area into sections.

If woodwork has good proportions, and door and window frames create a pleasing design, you can give them a natural finish. In some old houses, the woodwork is unusual and could be made a center of interest by using contrasting colors. When walls have a patterned paper with a number of different colors and values, it's better to use the predominant value for the woodwork.

The doors themselves, since they are part of the wall, generally should be painted the same color, unless they are to be made a point of interest. Frequently a contrasting door in halls, foyers, bathrooms, and kitchens can be particularly effective.

**Interior Paint and Wall Finishes.** Interior paints can be roughly categorized into one of three broad families: 1) flat paints that dry with no gloss and are most frequently used on walls and ceilings; 2) semi-gloss finishes (usually used in kitchens, bathrooms, and on woodwork generally) that are available in various lusters from a low satin finish to a very high gloss; and 3) the primers, sealers, and undercoats that are used as bases. All of these paints are available in different grades or qualities, and many in both solvent-thinned

**A floral pattern on a light background gives a cozy, cheery appearance.**

(mineral spirits, turpentine, or benzine) or water-thinned latex forms.

Flat latex interior paints are generally used for areas where there's little need for periodic washing and scrubbing; for example, living rooms, dining rooms, bedrooms, closets, and ceilings, since they cover well, are easy to apply, dry quickly, are almost odorless, and can be quickly and easily removed from applicators. Flat latex paints can be applied directly over semi-gloss and gloss enamel if the surface is first roughened with sandpaper or liquid sandpaper.

Flat alkyd and oil-based paints are often preferred for wood, wallboard, and metal surfaces, since they are more resistant to damage. In addition, they can be applied in thicker films to produce a more uniform appearance. They wash better than flat latex paints and are nearly odorless.

Semi-gloss enamels, including latex enamels, are usually preferred for kitchen, bathroom, laundry room, and similar work areas because they withstand intensive cleaning and wear. They form especially hard films, ranging from satin (semi-gloss) to a full-gloss finish.

For walls that are rough and have patched plaster, or to hide uneven seams in wallboard, a textured finish may be used. A special paint, thicker than ordinary paint, is used for this. A heavy coat of paint is applied to the wall surface and the desired texture added while the paint is still wet. Interesting textures can be achieved by the use of a brush, sponge, or a paint roller.

Penetrating oil finishes form durable and attractive finishes for interior wood surfaces such as wood paneling and trim. They seal the wood, forming tough, transparent films that will withstand frequent scrubbing and hard use, and are available in flat, semi-gloss or satin, and gloss finishes. Most natural varnishes are easily scratched, and the marks are difficult to conceal without redoing the entire surface. A good paste wax applied over the finished varnish will provide some protection against scratches. Synthetic polyurethane and epoxy varnishes are notable for durability and high resistance to stains, abrasions, acids and alkalis, solvents, strong cleaners, and chemicals.

## Wallcoverings

Wallcoverings (which include wallpaper) are one of the most versatile of all decorating devices. They can make a room appear cozy or formal, restful or active, gay or dignified. By careful selection of colors and patterns in a wallcovering, a room can be made to appear smaller or more spacious than it actually is. The

ceiling can be made to appear higher or lower according to the needs of the room, and wallcoverings can turn a dark gloomy room into a pleasant gay one. Certain types of wallcoverings seem to give more character and atmosphere to a room than do painted walls.

Before selecting a wallcovering, visit stores that have a wallcovering department and look through every book. As you look, try to visualize the paper on your own walls. Tilt the samples in a perpendicular line so that you can see the paper as it will appear on the walls. If possible, hold two rolls side by side to get the full effect of matching the patterns.

**Types of Wallcoverings.** Wallcoverings are available in almost any design you can think of. Floral patterns, scenics, plaids, stripes, vines, fruits, pastoral scenes, animals, birds or fowls, feather designs, geometrics, and modern abstracts are among the designs you will find. But not all wallcoverings have a pictorial pattern. Some have a textured appearance which looks like a fabric weave. Others are embossed. You'll also find a selection of good solid-colored papers. Special wallcoverings are made for the ceilings, and some of these harmonize in color with the sidewall patterns.

Companion wallcoverings, to be used in adjoining rooms, are also available. These wallcoverings have different designs, but the background color is the same. Companion wallcoverings may also be used in one room. A patterned covering may be used on one wall, and a solid matching-color covering on the other three walls. This is a good treatment for a long narrow room. The narrow end wall can be made to appear wider or to seemingly advance toward the center of the room.

Special features to look for in wallcoverings are washability, resistance to stains, and colorfastness. Some wallcoverings are more washable than others. Coverings for the kitchen or bathroom must be washable and resistant to steam vapor and grease stains.

Wallcoverings are available in many patterns, colors, and surface types. Because of these wide variations, you must observe certain precautions in decorating with them. Look at your room with a critical eye, and decide what character you want it to have. You must consider the personality of the person or persons who will use the room. Should your wallcovering have a pattern or be a solid color? If there are other areas of design in the room, walls probably should be plain. Too much design gives a feeling of activity and confusion.

Check the walls carefully to see if they're perfectly perpendicular to the floor and ceiling. If the walls are not perfectly straight, don't select a covering with a definite stripe or plaid pattern. An embossed covering or one with a small all-over design may be most suitable for walls with many imperfections. If you wish to give rooms in an old house a modern appearance, a distinctive weave pattern will provide a good background. A room crowded with furniture will appear more cluttered with patterned walls. Large designs and deep dark colors usually make a room appear smaller. Light solid colors and small designs make small rooms seem larger. Small delicate patterns may seem lost in large rooms.

Wallcoverings, of course, are available in various designs generally considered appropriate to the period of the furniture in your room. For instance, Provincial or Early American patterns are usually small florals, geometrics, plaids, and scenic papers; Pennsylvaniania Dutch colors are blue, yellow, or pink, with fruit, heart, bird, or stencil-type designs; French Provincial includes damask papers, floral stripes, floral medallions, *toiles de Jouy*; 18th-century styles—Queen Anne, Chippendale, Hepplewhite, Sheraton and Adam—call for more formal wallcoverings such as damasks, moire or brocaded velvet, small chintz patterns, and floral garlands in stripe effects. The Empire period of the 19th century contains Napoleonic emblems, figures, urns, swags, rosettes, and wreath motifs. Regency was a simpler era of formal stripes and swags. American Federal consists of wide stripes and panoramic scenes. Victorian style uses lavish, oversized florals. Modern decor has adopted stripes, checks, plaids, stylized flower motifs, and textured papers.

Many wallcoverings come in coordinates with drapery (and sometimes upholstery) fabrics. As a result, wall and window transitions can be smoother, creating the effect of space because there is no abrupt interruption. Coordinates can be picked up in the room as slipcovers or upholstery fabrics, thereby adding increased unity of design. Your color scheme, too, can be carried further, since wallpapers may feature colors that may be difficult to obtain in paints.

Wall hangings, such as pictures and textiles, show up to a greater advantage on plain walls. Extremely high ceilings can be made to appear lower by stopping the side wallcovering a foot or so below the ceiling and treating the rest of the wall the same as the ceiling. A horizontal striped pattern can give the same effect, while vertical stripes give the opposite effect. Select striped patterns with care; a covering with great contrast in color or value of the stripe and the background may become tiresome.

When selecting a wallcovering, consider activities that take place in a room. Quiet delicate designs and colors are more appropriate in rooms intended for

**An interesting combination of solid color and contrasting patterns.**

A bold wallcovering is more appropriate in an active room such as the dining room.

sleeping, resting, reading, and conversation. The living room and bedrooms usually fall into this category. For more active rooms, such as the den and family room, bolder and more vivid designs and colors may be used. Because the entry and the dining room usually are not occupied for long periods of time, they may have more outstanding patterns and colors. Kitchen walls should be cheerful and restful. But avoid a spotty scattered pattern and the too realistic designs that copy nature in every detail. A conventionalized or stylized design in the kitchen is more satisfactory over a long period of time.

As with painted walls, consider woodwork as a part of the background and avoid great contrasts between the color and value of the woodwork and the wallcovering. Contrasting colors emphasize the woodwork and tend to break the room into different areas of walls, windows, and doors. Painting woodwork the same color as the background or the predominant color in the wallcovering helps to tie the woodwork and walls together and make a unified background for the room furnishings.

Well-designed wallcovering may be the source of a color scheme for a room, and it can tie together all the colors used in a room. Wallcovering for a room should be harmonious in color and design with that of other areas that open into it. In selecting wallcovering for the ceiling, remember that a light-colored ceiling reflects more light than a dark one. A glossy-surfaced covering will produce more glare than will a soft, nonglossy covering.

**Wallcovering Murals.** From the time of the earliest cave drawings and Grecian frescoes to the present, wall murals have been a distinctive element of home decorating. Today, more varied, more useful, more available than ever before, they provide the homemaker with stimulating, colorful, and practical ideas.

The words "wallcovering murals" include many types—scenics, panels, supergraphics, abstracts, evocations of design themes from nature, and scenes from all over the world. What can these murals do for your walls? A major plus is perspective—they are

often designed to act as "window walls," visually changing the dimensions (horizontal and vertical), giving the illusion of depth, or "opening up" the room by means of the view shown, the colors, and the architectural features built into the mural itself. Murals can also pull rooms together, turn corners, and blend panels and backgrounds. Most mural sets come with additional background to use on longer and adjacent walls. In addition, murals provide instant guides to the colors of carpeting, upholstery, and accessories. And, of course, the murals set the period, the atmosphere, the design era, and particular ambiance that suits you.

Wallcovering murals present no difficulty in hanging; the planning of where and at what height they're to be hung is the biggest part of the job. (In many museums and art galleries, the paintings are hung lower than they formerly were. Presumably this gives a more contemporary and intimate look, as well as adding height to the room.) The furniture you use in conjunction with panels or a mural will determine at what level you want the interest centered. Just remember to relate any murals or panels to your furnishings as if they were pictures, and don't "sky" them.

**Special Wallcoverings.** There are several other types of wallcoverings that can be used to beautify your home:

*Flocked* patterns are among the oldest and newest in existence. In recent years, flocking has been added to almost any surface where it will stick, but it still appears most widely in damask-type patterns that simulate cut velvet. Flocks need a little more preparation than the average wallcovering. In the first place, it's best to use a lining paper with flocks, as the raised flocking reflects extra light and betrays any unevenness of the wall. Second, flocks require the use of special, non-cellulose paste, and this must be prevented from getting on the flocked surface.

*Foil* and *mylar* wallcoverings are comparatively new

developments. Very thin sheets of gold, silver, and aluminum leaf—long used in the decoration of interiors and objects—led to the making of metallic papers from powder. These could be "polished" to a high shine, but foil coverings are gradually superseding most metallic powders because of their superior brightness.

Because of their reflectiveness, foils create depth and help brighten rooms, but foils can be overpowering and should be used rather sparingly. Too much foil will distract from the realism you want to convey in your rooms. They are especially attuned to contemporary-themed houses, although they work well with most other types of decor, too. For instance, they are good on a dining-room wall or in a powder room where there is no window, hence a need for brightness. But foils should never be used in a kitchen or a child's room. Foil is too formal, and it won't stand up to abuse. Another problem with foils is that they magnify wall imperfections; so be sure the walls in your house are prepared properly before any foil wallcovering is installed.

Actually, foils are a thin sheet of metal on a paper or cloth backing. In spite of their strength, they need to be hung (as do flocks) over a thoroughly dried-out lining paper, and each sheet of foil, after being pasted

**Wood planking produces a rustic effect.**

with a special adhesive, should be allowed from five to seven minutes "rest" for absorption and softening before hanging.

*Natural* wallcoverings—burlaps, grasscloth, hemp, leather, and cork—are becoming popular, especially for entry halls. They add warmth and extend a psychological welcome. The naturals also work well in dens and studies because they radiate comfort and security. For the same reasons, you might want to install grasscloth in a master bedroom. Natural wallcoverings generally have a paper backing and are hung much like other wallcoverings.

*Vinyl-coated* papers or cloths are the most popular of today's wallcoverings. They're durable, scrubbable, and resistant to damage; so they are the best choices for hard-wear areas like kitchens, baths, laundry rooms, and children's bedrooms.

You'll get maximum impact by installing vinyls on four walls of a room. (But be careful; remember that dark-colored wallcoverings can visually shrink a room.) Or you can use the vinyls on a single wall as an accent or to help establish a theme. For example, a print of old skillets and other utensils would be ideal for a country kitchen.

Vinyls are hung much like ordinary paper wallcoverings and are available in most of the same

patterns—floral patterns, geometric, etc. In addition, vinyls can be had that give the modern "wet look." Many of the new coverings are available prepasted, which makes the project ideal for a "do-it-yourselfer." The so-called strippable coverings—a backing paper is peeled off and the covering pressed on the wall—are also easy to install.

**Planking and Paneling**

Wall backgrounds consist of materials other than those of covered or painted surfaces. Among the foremost of these are paneling and planking.

**Solid-Wood Planking.** Various types and patterns of woods are available for application on walls to obtain the desired decorative effects. For informal treatment, knotty pine, redwood, whitepocket Douglas fir, sound wormy chestnut, and pecky cypress, with a natural finish or stained and varnished, may be used to cover one or more walls of a room. In addition, such desirable hardwoods as red oak, pecan, elm, walnut, white oak, and cherry also are available. Most solid-wood planking comes in thicknesses from 3/8 to 3/4 inch; widths vary from 4 to 8 inches; lengths from 3 to 10 feet.

When using wood planking remember that if you wish to accent a wall, use boards of random widths; to subdue a wall use boards of equal width. Small rooms can be made to appear longer by applying the wood horizontally. Of course, it can be applied vertically,

**An example of foil wall papering.**

horizontally, diagonally, or in various directions.

**Plywood Panels.** Plywood panels come in a wide range of faces varying from richly figured real-wood oak, mahogany, birch, and walnut, to fir and pine. There are also some printed-faced plywoods. Thus, plywood allows a full choice of decorative material to meet every taste and budget. They can work effectively in either traditional or modern interiors. One outstanding advantage of using plywood paneling is the elimination of periodic redecorating. The only upkeep required is an occasional waxing.

The illustration here suggests a few interesting ways to arrange panels in architecturally and decoratively correct designs. Many of these can be used on all the walls in a room; others are intended to create a point of interest or contrast in one part of the room only. In the latter cases the rest of the walls may be covered with complete panels of plywood in natural finish, or with less expensive or lower-grade plywood. Plywood panels can also be used in combination with painted or papered walls, or with glass, masonry, and other materials.

**Hardboard Panels.** Hardboard manufactured for use as prefinished paneling is specifically treated for resistance to stains, scrubbing, and moisture. It's also highly resistant to dents, mars, and scuffs. In some cases, the face simulates wood grains such as walnut, cherry, birch, oak, teak, and pecan—and in a variety of shades. It may be smooth-surfaced or random-grooved. In addition, there are the decorative and work-saving plastic-surfaced hardboards which resist water, stains, and household chemicals exceptionally

**Various types of hardboard panels.**

**Simulated brick looks like the real thing.**

well. A typical surface consists of baked-on plastic. Most hardboard is sufficiently dense and moisture-resistant for use in bathrooms, kitchens, and laundry rooms. The variety of finishes and sizes is extensive. In addition to rich-looking wood grains, finishes include marble reproductions, plain colors, speckled colors, simulated tile, marble and brick, barn siding, lace prints, wallpaper textures, and murals. Vinyl-clad panels are also available in decorative and wood-grain finishes.

**Insulation Board or Fiberboard.** Insulation board, or fiberboard, is available in the form of planks and sheets. The plank is 8, 12, or 16 inches wide by 8, 10, 12, or 14 feet long. The sheet is 4 or 8 feet wide by 6, 7, 8, 9, 10, 12, or 14 feet long. Both are usually prefinished by the manufacturer with such wallcoverings as burlap, grasscloth, cork, leather, and vinyl.

### Other Wallcovering Materials

In addition to the so-called standard wallcoverings—paint, wallpaper, paneling, and planking—there is a wide range of other materials that can be used. They include many types of tile, glass, stone and brick—both real and simulated.

**Ceramic Tiles.** There are many types of ceramic tiles, including glazed wall tiles, ceramic mosaics, quarry tiles, and specialty tiles, and they're available in a wide range of designs and colors. Tiles range in size from 1-inch-square mosaics to 12-inch squares, and are available in high- or low-relief designs with colorful glazes or multicolored patterns. There are also handsome contoured tiles. Along with hexagons, octagons, and rectangles, there are curvilinear shapes inspired by historic Moorish designs, houses in Normandy, and villas in Florence. Many of these are quarry tiles, which are now offered in a large range of natural colors as well as durable glazes. Because of the many practical and decorative virtues uniquely its own, tile has a place on any wall in your home.

Other tile materials include plastic, metal, and cork. The latter is quite popular for small sections of walls that are to be used as points of interest. Plastic tile has never been too popular, while the metal type is usually limited to use on kitchen walls that are apt to be splattered by grease.

**Simulated Brick and Stone.** For interior use, simulated plastic brick and stone are inexpensive, easy to install, and, in most cases, look like the real thing. In addition to their decorative value, these textured wall surfaces can be installed without having to add bracing to the floor or a step to the foundation, which would be necessary with real brick or stone because

of the weight.

Simulated brick and stone are made of various plastic materials; styrene, urethane, and rigid vinyl are the most common. Some are fire resistant and may be used to surround fireplaces. Simulated brick and stone are highly durable and come in a wide variety of colors and styles. Some are sold in sheet form, others, individually. They can even be obtained already applied to plywood or hardboard.

**Mirroring.** While virtually everyone knows about the "looking-glass" function and typical decorative uses of mirrors, many homeowners overlook their total potential. Properly employed, mirrors are capable of expanding space, multiplying beauty, camouflaging structural flaws, and, in many other ways, supplying a unique visual element that offers almost magical solutions to various "knotty" decorating problems.

Basically, the feeling of depth that a mirror supplies gives a feeling of space where little exists. In problem rooms this means walls can be visually moved outward, ceilings pushed upward, and space generally manipulated at will. If an area tends to be too long and narrow, a mirrored sidewall visually broadens the corridor. If a room is short and boxy, a mirrored end wall extends the depth. And in rooms with low ceilings, there's no better way to raise the roof, visually, than to butt a mirror against the ceiling line.

Ordinarily, we think of a mirror's reflection as a doubling effect. In many cases, however, it's an even higher multiplier. By mirroring two adjacent walls of a small bath, for example, the apparent room dimensions are quadrupled, not doubled. While this technique should be used judiciously to avoid a busy confused effect, it can often be worked to advantage in confined areas such as a bath or foyer.

In addition to multiplying space, mirrors also can create pleasant duplications of an important accessory. A decorative wall sconce, for example, when mounted on a mirror, becomes an unusual twin decorative device. A bell-shaped chandelier mounted flush on a mirrored ceiling becomes a dazzling crystal globe. And in an instance such as this, the elegant effect of the crystal sphere is achieved at half the cost of the larger chandelier that the mirror implies is there.

A home decorator who thinks of modern mirrors as merely clear, silvered "looking glasses" is missing the full potential in color, pattern, texture, and styling variations today's production processes make possible. If it appears that a clear mirror would be too bright or harsh for a certain installation, the decorator can select a mirror made from a modern tinted plate glass. Unlike the colored glasses of the past, today's neutral gray and bronze hues do not distort color values. They merely provide a handsome, muted effect while still reflecting the true colors of a room's decor. Improved production techniques also are responsible for a revival of the antique mirror. The smoky, shadowy effects possible today are startling in themselves, but these effects can be further heightened by applying a random veining in one or more of a variety of colors.

**Moldings.** Decorative moldings can be used to emphasize the beauty of a wall as well as helping to modify the size of a room. Wood moldings are made in various shapes and sizes. They can be applied vertically, horizontally, or diagonally, can be used to accent windows, and to frame sections of wallcovering.

## FLOORS

Fine flooring has been a symbol of luxurious living since the days when noblemen and kings walked on marble and rich parquetry. Today, floors are more important than ever in the decorating scheme—but wealth is no longer a prerequisite for enjoying luxury underfoot.

The choice of floor coverings is categorized into two basic types: soft (carpeting and rugs), and hard (wood, flagstone, brick, ceramic tile, and various resilient surfaces). Let's first look at soft-material floorings.

### Carpeting and Rugs

Carpets and rugs can be the canvas upon which you paint your total room design, or they can be a striking bold splash of color that speaks for itself. Whether you choose wall-to-wall carpeting, room-size rugs, or area rugs, depends upon your needs and your life style. You may know you're going to move soon, in which case you'll want rugs that can move with you. You may have beautiful wood floors or existing carpeting and merely want to accent areas with rugs. Or you may want the permanence and warmth of installed wall-to-wall luxury.

Carpets and rugs, of course, insulate your floors against sound and extreme temperatures. They give your rooms a luxurious look and feel which emphasize your taste in furnishings.

**Carpet Fibers.** All carpets consist of surface pile and backing. Surface pile may be made of natural or manmade fibers such as:

*Wool*, the traditional natural fiber, is resilient, luxurious, resistant to abrasion and soil, warm, and easy to maintain. It is generally higher in cost per square yard than the man-made fibers (acrylic, nylon, polyester, and polypropylene).

*Acrylic* fibers are most nearly like wool in appearance. An acrylic carpet is a good choice if you want the look and feel of wool at a lower cost and with hypoallergenic properties (having a relatively low capacity to induce hypersensitivity). Modacrylic is sometimes used alone in bathroom and/or in scatter rugs, and in larger carpets it is blended with acrylic because the modacrylic's self-extinguishing properties increase flame resistance.

*Nylon.* Soil resistance or soil-hiding characteristics of this fiber are poor to excellent, depending upon the particular nylon fiber and how it's used. It has good resilience, excellent wear resistance, and good colorfastness. Nylon carpet made from short fibers, instead of continuous filaments, may fuzz under hard wear. Static electricity when humidity is low is a problem with some nylons, but newer types are available that are static free.

*Polyester.* This manmade fiber has a soft, luxurious appearance, good wear resistance, and colorfastness. Its resilience is somewhat less than nylon, so denser pile construction is needed for the same performance. Abrasion-resistant, low static tendencies, and high ease-of-care properties are other characteristics of polyester fabrics.

*Polypropylene or Olefin.* This fiber is generally used for indoor-outdoor and commercial use because it's not damaged by moisture. It also has good wear and abrasion resistance, excellent resistance to water-based stains, excellent colorfastness, and like the other man-made fabrics, it naturally resists moths and beetles.

Two or more fibers are frequently blended in carpet surface yarns to take advantage of the outstanding characteristics of each. For example, a blend of 70 per cent wool and 30 per cent nylon looks and feels like wool, but has some of the toughness of nylon. A carpet label must show the percentage by weight of each fiber. Less than 20 per cent of any fiber wouldn't be enough to affect carpet quality, and would have been added merely as a selling point.

It must be remembered that fibers are used not only to make surface yarns, but also to make backings that hold the surface yarns together. Here are some of the more popular fibers for this use:

*Jute* is a plant fiber used in backings for woven and tufted carpets. It is strong, durable, and resilient. Jute also absorbs and retains adhesives well to help bonding between layers of the backing in tufted carpets. It may mildew in excessively damp locations.

*Cotton* is used in some woven backings. It is durable and strong, but may mildew in excessively moist locations.

*Kraftcord.* This fiber is specially processed from wood pulp. It is sturdy, but not as durable as other backing materials, and may mildew. Some Kraft fiber is now being treated with a special vinyl bath to make it mildew resistant and more durable.

*Rayon* is strong and durable, and is used in some woven carpets.

*Polypropylene or Olefin (Synthetic jute).* This man-made fiber is used as backing in tufted carpets. It is strong and durable and resists mildew.

*Rubber and Vinyl.* These materials are sometimes substituted for the usual secondary backing of tufted carpet. They provide additional resilience and help prevent the carpet from stretching or wrinkling. They are also less expensive than most of the other materials.

*Padding.* Padding (underlay) will lengthen carpet life by helping to absorb crushing forces on the pile. It also adds underfoot comfort and further insulation against noise, heat, and cold. Some carpets are made with sponge or latex padding permanently attached, while others require separate padding. The two most popular types are listed below and are available in grades for light, medium, and heavy traffic conditions.

*Felted.* This padding is made of animal hair, jute fibers, or any combination thereof. Some is coated with rubber. It is sturdy under foot. Felted pads, however, tend to mat, and can mildew if exposed to continued wetness.

*Rubber or Urethane.* This padding of latex foam, sponge rubber, or bonded urethane (which is stronger than virgin urethane) is available as a cushion, or frequently has a fiber facing on one side to keep it from stretching. Neither type is affected by humidity nor attracts vermin.

**Carpet Texture.** There is a great variety of carpet textures. Since furniture styles are being mixed today, however, you're not bound to an all-traditional or all-modern style of carpeting, unless that is your preference. The standard textures you are most likely to find are the following:

*Level-loop Pile.* This is an uncut loop of yarn of uniform height which forms the carpet surface. This texture wears well and tends to hide footprints, but it shows dust and lint readily. It's easier to vacuum than uneven textures.

*Level-tip Shear.* The surface of this texture is level,

**Wall-to-wall carpeting gives a plush, rich feeling to a room.**

with some loops cut and some uncut. It tends to show dirt and lint readily, but hides footprints better than plush, although not as well as level-loop pile. It's easier to vacuum than uneven textures.

*Multilevel-loop Pile.* All yarns with this texture are uncut loops, and the loops are of several different levels. This texture hides footprints, dust, and dirt better than level-loop carpets, but it takes more strokes of a vacuum to clean it.

*Random Shear.* This is similar to the multilevel loop, except that the highest level of loops is cut. It hides footprints, dust, and dirt well, but is harder to vacuum than level pile.

*Cut Pile and Plush.* These are the richest looking of the textures. All yarn loops are cut so that yarns stand upright and form an even surface. They are easier to clean than uneven textures, but tend to show dirt and lint readily. They are also subject to shading when yarns are bent, making them reflect light in different directions. This is often undesirable, and it can be reduced by vacuuming the carpet in one direction.

*Sculptured or Carved.* With this texture, the pile yarns are sheared at different levels to make a design. It hides footprints, dust, and dirt well, but is harder to vacuum than level pile.

*Shag.* With this informal texture, the pile yarns 1 ½ inches and longer are either looped or cut. The pile has a random, tumbled appearance. It hides footprints, dust, and dirt, but may be difficult to vacuum.

*Frieze or Twist.* The yarns of this texture are tightly twisted and sometimes heat set to increase resilience and durability and to give a nubby appearance. It wears well and hides footprints, dirt, and dust. If it has a level surface, it's not difficult to clean.

Generally, with all carpet textures, the greater the density, the better the quality and the longer the carpet will wear. A brush of the hand over the surface of the pile will indicate if it is thick, tight, and springy. Folding a corner of the carpet will reveal how much backing shows through the pile, though this test may not be valid for shag carpet. A short or mediun height dense pile will wear best in traffic areas.

**Rugs.** The terms carpet and rug are often used interchangeably and loosely by the layman; however, there's a technical difference. The difference is not in the texture or materials, but in the manner in which the edges are finished and the design. For instance, standard rug sizes range from 1 ½ by 5 feet to 24 by 36 feet. Larger sizes would be special order. Carpeting, on the other hand, comes in rolls ranging in width from 22 ½ inches for halls and stairs, to more conventional widths of 12 and 15 feet for rooms, with a few stores stocking special textures up to 30 feet wide. Incidentally, the term "broadloom" applies to carpets woven in widths 54 inches or wider, as distinguished from narrow-loom widths of 22 ½, 27, and 36 inches.

The edges of a rug are bound on all four sides. Sometimes the warp threads are tied and knotted into a fringe at the two ends. Carpeting is bound, however, only on two sides, leaving the ends unfinished to allow for cutting the desired length.

In carpeting, the design is an all-over pattern, comparable to that of yard goods or wallcovering, and similarly matched when strips are laid to cover a wide area. A rug, on the other hand, is a complete unit. Actually, room-size rugs are very practical; they can be turned so they wear evenly and you can send them out for professional cleaning. If you buy a good rug, it should last for years and you can usually use it more easily when you move than wall-to-wall carpeting. It's also possible to change color schemes more easily by moving rugs from one room to another. Area rugs are now being used over carpeting for a decorator effect, or in areas of heavy traffic.

Carpet tiles in one-foot-square sizes are used for kitchens and bathrooms. Usually they have a foam backing that holds the woven fabric in place and acts as built-in padding. And if one is burned or permanently stained, you can replace it rather than buy a new rug.

**Oriental Rugs.** Colorful, hand-woven Oriental rugs in a variety of colors and intricate designs are experiencing renewed popularity. Authentic antique rugs more than 50 years old sell for thousands of dollars at auctions and galleries, and new Oriental rugs imported from the Middle East and India also cost a

great deal. Several carpet manufacturers, however, are creating copies of Oriental rugs and offering them at prices suitable for the average family. Although these rugs are made on power looms, they reflect the same colors and designs that have made rugs from the exotic lands of Central Asia popular for centuries.

The intricate patterns woven from knotted, sheared wool, cotton, or rug silk, first reached Europe from the Far East, India, Turkey, Persia (Iran), Samarkand and Pakistan during the Renaissance. The rugs covered tables and walls. Occasionally, a rug even found its way to the floor. During the 1920s and '30s, Oriental or Persian rugs were popular floor coverings in American homes.

Iran and Turkey are the major centers for handwoven Oriental rugs today. Of course, modern machinery has almost eliminated the need for hand knotting and weaving in these countries, too. And prices have gone up, as the weavers demand better wages to keep pace with today's economy.

**Rug and Carpet Color.** Carpet color can be your most versatile ally in decorating, and is one of the first considerations you'll have in choosing a soft floor covering. Lighting affects color, so if at all possible, arrange to view your carpet color in both the daytime and nighttime lighting your room will receive.

A wisely chosen multicolored carpet or rug makes an otherwise plain color scheme seem more interesting. For sheer beauty, when expertly selected, they can be your decorative scheme. From a practical standpoint, multicolored floor coverings disguise signs of soil and wear. They are most frequently used in corridors and foyers where traffic is heavy, and in a dining room where food spots are prevalent.

The modern eye is more accustomed to seeking satisfaction in mass and textures and restful colors than in elaborate detail and designs. A rug in one color—either textured or with the faintest pattern clipped or woven into the pile—is usually easier to live with for a long period of time. Furniture can be effectively displayed, and choice of upholstery and drapery fabrics isn't so restricted. The feeling of space in a room is preserved or increased by the absence of a distracting design. Spaciousness also is achieved with wall-to-wall carpeting, although at greater cost, and by using rugs in color values flattering to the tone of the surrounding wood floor.

When selecting the color of rugs and/or carpeting, remember that warm colors react just as they do in walls and fabrics. Since they have advancing qualities they don't help to increase room size. However, they do add warmth and vitality. Thus, use warm colors to make a room look smaller, or to make a sunless room cozier.

The cool colors won't give the vigor to a drab room that the warm colors will give; but they're restful, spacious, and an excellent foil for brilliance in the upholstery. Speaking of upholstery, when it and the floor covering are the same color, make sure that there is textural difference between the two so that they don't melt into each other, sacrificing the beauty of the furniture contours.

**Beautiful wooden floors should be shown off rather than covered with carpeting.**

74

Shades of color also create illusions. The powerful pales recede and make a room look larger, while the deep tones seem to bring the walls together. Pale or light shades soil faster than those of middle value, but are practical in a room which doesn't have direct traffic from outside doors. On the whole, light shades are not as impractical as you might think, and as they soil, they gray down fairly evenly. Dark tones, on the other hand, show foot tracks more readily than do colors of middle value. A deep blue, brown, or black shows every speck of dirt on it, especially in a plush texture. If you're going to use a very dark tone on the floor, select a rug or carpet with an uneven surface or a pebbly hard twist surface.

## Wood Floors

Wood floors were probably first used in the mid-11th century, and have been the leading hard surface flooring ever since. True, through the years they've been elaborated to the elegance of intricate parquetry and inlaid floral designs, complicated basket weaves, or herring-bone effects. But floors, along with other decorative details, have reverted to simplicity. The popular wood floor today is of either the random-width hardwood boards, prevalent in Early American and Colonial homes, or the regulation narrow hardwood flooring seen everywhere.

Hardwood floors have a natural beauty which should be emphasized and protected by the finish. There are two basic types of floor finishes from which to choose: penetrating seals and surface coatings.

Penetrating seals (with or without stain) soak into the flooring material to form a strong bond with the wood. When you add a good paste or solvent-based liquid wax and buff well, the result is a tough floor with a beautiful gloss. Both the wood and the sealer are worn away at the same time, leaving little evidence of wear. When necessary, heavy traffic areas can be repaired with sealer and the floor will not appear spot finished.

The surface coating group includes shellac, varnish, polyurethane, epoxy, and amino resin.

Shellac is the oldest and cheapest of these finishes, and it doesn't wear as well as the others, especially under heavy traffic. Natural varnish will also wear well under light use, but won't withstand heavy abrasion or abuse. In addition, varnish scratches white, making it less desirable in appearance. Natural varnish is seldom used today.

Polyurethane, epoxy, and amino resin finishes (plastic or synthetic varnish finishes) are tough, long wearing, resistant to chemicals, and quick drying.

They are also resistant to the scratching and marring that are readily apparent with shellac and natural varnish.

Painted floors are effective, especially in keeping with a provincial American feel or where the traffic pattern is covered with throw-rugs. But be sure to use a fast-drying polyurethane floor enamel to obtain the hard finish necessary for wood floors. Other types of floor enamels can also be used, but unless recommended for wood floors, they may be too soft and slow-drying, or too hard and brittle.

A spattered effect is an interesting variation. After the floor is painted a solid color, choose one or two other contrasting colors. Dip a dry paintbrush in one color, and hit it gently against the palm of your hand so the paint spatters in droplets. Cover the entire floor surface. Let this spatter dry, then spatter it with another color. You'll have an unusual, gay surface that won't show dirt or heel marks.

## Resilient Flooring

Practicality, convenience, ease of application and care (no waxing), and long wear are a few of the reasons why resilient flooring continues to be one of the most popular choices of homeowners everywhere. With the tremendous variety of materials, designs, and colors available, it is possible to create just about any floor scheme that strikes your fancy. For example, you can install a floor of a single color, or you can combine different colorings into a custom floor design that matches room requirements and individual taste. If your decorating taste leans to the natural look, you will find countless resilient materials that closely resemble slate, brick, ceramic tile, mosaic, wood, terrazzo, marble, and stone. Many of these floors feature an embossed surface texture that adds a striking note to the design.

**Types of Resilient Floors.** Resilient floors are manufactured in two basic types: (a) sheet materials; and (b) tiles. The latter are cemented in place to serve as a permanent floor. Sheet materials are also cemented in place, but some can be installed loosely like rugs. Tiles generally come in 9- or 12-inch squares; sheet materials are available in continuous rolls up to 12 feet wide.

Here's a rundown of various resilient floor coverings and their performance characteristics:

| Material | Backing | How installed | Where to install | Ease of installation | Resilience and maintenance | Durability | Quietness |
|---|---|---|---|---|---|---|---|
| **TILE MATERIALS** | | | | | | | |
| Asphalt | None | Adhesive | Anywhere | Fair | Difficult | Fair | Very poor |
| Vinyl asbestos | None | Adhesive | Anywhere | Easy | Very easy | Excellent | Poor |
| Vinyl | None | Adhesive | Anywhere | Easy | Easy | Good—excellent | Fair |
| Rubber | None | Adhesive | Anywhere | Fair | Easy | Good | Good |
| Cork | None | Adhesive | On or above grade | Fair | Fair (with vinyl, good) | Good | Excellent |
| **SHEET MATERIALS** | | | | | | | |
| Inlaid vinyl | Felt | Adhesive | Above grade | Fair | Easy | Good | Fair |
| | Foam and felt | Adhesive | Above grade | Difficult | Easy | Good | Good |
| | Asbestos | Adhesive | Anywhere | Very difficult | Easy | Excellent | Fair |
| | Foam | Adhesive | Anywhere | Very difficult | Easy | Excellent | Good |
| Printed vinyl | Felt | Loose-lay | Above grade | Easy | Fair | Poor | Poor |
| | Felt | Adhesive | Above grade | Fair | Easy | Fair | Poor |
| | Foam and felt | Loose-lay | Above grade | Easy | Easy | Fair | Good |
| | Foam and asbestos | Adhesive or loose-lay | Anywhere | Fair—easy | Easy | Good | Good |
| | Foam | Loose-lay | Anywhere | Easy | Easy | Good | Good |

**Custom Effects With Resilient Floors.** When using resilient floor materials, there are innumerable effects that can be produced by combining patterned flooring with feature strips. These are narrow strips (available in various widths), which come in a wide range of neutrals and decorator colors such as avocado green, turquoise, bold blue, misty purple, Chinese red, and burnt orange.

You can also achieve an inexpensive custom effect in your floors by utilizing ready-made insets. Designs include compasses, eagles, sunbursts, roosters, and floral bouquets. Special effects can be created with standard hand-cut insets such as monograms or script initials, or with custom insets designed to your individual order. A skillful flooring specialist can duplicate almost any example of visual art—from a sketch of your favorite sailboat to the silhouette of your child's pet dog. A custom inset can even repeat a design element from a special fabric or a treasured wall hanging.

With resilient floorings, you can achieve exactly the decor you desire. Make use of modern techniques to create these special effects:

1. A gentle "S" curve joining two harmonious shades of sheet vinyl gives visual sweep to a room.

2. An elongated design, created with feature strips, can lead the eye to a view, or broaden a narrow room.

3. Tiles set diagonally and outlined with decorator strips or narrow metal inlay will highlight a corner fireplace.

4. A shaped border can dramatize the setting of dining table and chairs or call attention to a particularly lovely piece of furniture.

Area rugs lend exciting contrast, in both color and texture, to a resilient floor. Use a patterned rug on a plain floor, or vice versa. Shaped accent rugs—round, hexagonal, and free-form—or those with fringed borders, are especially decorative.

A change in flooring color or the use of inset strips can be used to differentiate the children's play area from the bar section in a recreation room, or the work area from family area in a kitchen/family room.

A floor design featuring two or more colors can repeat the color scheme of the entire room and give a pleasing balance to the over-all decor. Brick-patterned flooring, continuing up the front of a built-in bench, gives the look of actual masonry.

Make sure you consider the period and style of your furniture before choosing a resilient floor. Whatever your decor, there's a floor that will enhance it. Here's a general guide:

*Traditional*-parquet, cork, or the terrazzo or marble look.

*Mediterranean*-Spanish tiles, either shaped or patterned, or hexagonal tiles.

*Early American*-brick, slate, or tile designs.

*Contemporary*-flagstone, slate, stone-chip look.

*French or Italian Provincial*-terrazzo, mosaic, tile, or brick.

## Hard Floor Surfaces

In special locations within the home, hard floor materials such as "real" ceramic tile, slate, flagstone, and brick may be used. In fact, ceramic tile is one of the oldest floor-covering materials; it dates back almost 7,000 years.

There are three types of ceramic tiles in common use today; quarry tiles, ceramic mosaics, and glazed tiles. The last are usually a little thinner than glazed wall tiles, but are made in various sizes and shapes and a variety of designs and colors. Some are so perfectly glazed that they form a monochromatic surface. Others have a softer, natural shade variation within each unit and from tile to tile. In addition, ceramic floors can be bright-glazed, matte-glazed, or unglazed. There are also extra-duty glazed floor tiles suitable for heavy-traffic areas.

Ceramic mosaics are available in 1-by-1- and 2-by-

**With resilient floorings, you can choose from an almost infinite array of decorating effects.**

2-inch squares, and come with or without a glaze. In addition to the standard units, they are available in a wide assortment of colors and shapes. Mosaics are usually sold mounted in 1-by-1- and 1-by-2-foot sheets for easy installation.

Quarry tiles, which also are made from natural ceramic materials, are available in a variety of colors; the most common types are in shades of red, chocolate, and buff. They come in shapes ranging from square to Spanish forms.

Slate tiles, flagstone, and marble slabs are available in random shapes, or can be purchased in geometric shapes—usually squares and rectangles. They are available in green, red, purple, gray, and black. Because of cost, however, the use of slate and flagstone is usually limited to small areas such as foyers and entryways.

Brick floors are becoming increasingly popular as a handsome and eye-catching element inside a home. A wide selection of brick colors and sizes is available to the homeowner. Special bricks known as "pavers" are generally used in floors, patios, and walkways. Pavers are even more wear resistant than standard bricks, and they are thinner, usually about 1½ inches thick. The thinner bricks reduce the floor's weight and are used where the added thickness isn't needed. Standard bricks, however, may be used in any home.

## CEILINGS

Things are definitely "looking up" in decorating circles. Ceilings, for a long time completely ignored and painted a flat white, are once again coming into prominence. True, you can't use ceilings in the way that you can walls or floors, but you certainly can put ceilings to work; and you must if you intend to carry out your decorating plan. If you overlook the ceilings, the chances are that your home will never seem quite right to you.

There are only a few decorative rules for ceilings, and they are exacting, for ceilings are more than just covering surfaces. In contemporary homes, ceilings

may be the pivot or balance wheel (if they may be described as that) on which your color plans depend. For example, to do the most efficient job to improve a room's lighting, ceilings must be plain—little or no interfering ornamentation, moldings, recesses, or similar architectural obstructions. They should be as flat finished as you can make them. Hard-white painted ceilings are the best light reflectors; nonetheless, they are usually uninteresting and often unpleasant. Flat reflecting surfaces should carry a hint, at the very least, of some color, so that reflected light is warmed, enlivened, and picks up a glow. What color you use will depend upon your color scheme. Light tints or shades of the wall color, the floor coverings, or the drapery background are the most suitable. You achieve greater decorative unity without sacrificing ceiling efficiency.

In little-used rooms, ceilings may be pulled down in color value to that of the walls, and this could be decoratively desirable. Foyers, hallways, and occasionally bedrooms can use a deeper, richer ceiling color to increase their decorative interest, provided good lighting qualities are not destroyed.

A patterned wallpaper or fabric that carries out the room's theme can be dramatic overhead and is a newer trend in decorating. Choose a geometric or any other design with no direction, so the pattern looks right from any part of the room. Stripes, if used, must meet at a central location. Other materials sometimes used on ceilings include various matting, caning, and treillage effects.

**This slanted, beamed ceiling adds to the atmosphere of warmth.**

Today, many homes are designed with cathedral ceilings, or have a vaulted appearance. Skylights are also becoming more popular in residential architectural design. And, of course, beamed ceilings are an old favorite in Early American designs. Incidentally, if you wish to have a beamed ceiling, ready-made, ready-to-install beams are available at most lumber dealers. They are made of solid lumber, plywood, polyurethane plastic foam, or metal. The number of beams and patterns employed depends on the size of the room and personal preference. Some ceilings will appear best with the beams running in one direction only, while others look fine with crossed beams.

Of course, if you're planning remodeling along with your redecorating project, many of the wall materials—plywood, hardboard, etc.—may be used on ceilings. Most popular, however, are the so-called "acoustical" tiles or panels. Available in many attractive patterns and designs, some of the tiles or panels can be installed with "invisible" seams. Acoustical ceilings are ideal for special rooms—kitchens, game rooms, family rooms, and music rooms—because of their sound-trapping characteristics. With a grid-type ceiling, translucent plastic panels can be installed to aid in light control. Grid ceilings are also the easiest way to obtain a dropped ceiling, which may add a new beauty to a room—particularly in remodeled houses where a lower ceiling seems more in scale or where ugly beams can be hidden.

| Period Style | Associated Styles | Walls & Ceilings | Floors | Floor Coverings |
|---|---|---|---|---|
| Early English Tudor Jacobean Charles II | Italian Renaissance Spanish Renaissance William & Mary Larger pieces of Queen Anne | Oak panels Rough plaster with oak trim Parquetry ceilings | Hardwood stained, dark strips and planks on flooring Stone, Tiles | Oriental and large-patterned domestic rugs Plain rugs |
| Anglo-Dutch William & Mary Queen Anne | Chippendale Early Georgian Louis XVI Smaller pieces of Jacobean, such as gate-leg table or Windsor chair | Papered Painted (in light tones) Hung with fabrics Paneled | Hardwood flooring Parquetry | Oriental and large-patterned domestic rugs Plain rugs |
| Early Georgian Chippendale | Chippendale Early Georgian Louis XVI Smaller pieces of Jacobean, such as gate-leg table or Windsor chair | Painted dado Painted Paneled Papered upper section | Hardwood flooring Parquetry | Plain or small-patterned rugs or carpets Oriental rugs |
| Late Georgian Adam Hepplewhite Sheraton Empire Federal | Chinese Chippendale Louis XVI Duncan Phyfe Directoire | Plain plaster Painted Papered Large wood panels painted Gesso ceilings | Hardwood flooring Parquetry | Plain or small-patterned rugs or carpets Oriental rugs |
| Louis XIV, XV, and XVI | All late Georgian styles 1 or 2 pieces of Directoire | Large wood panels painted and decorated Wallpaper in Chinese motifs | Hardwood flooring Parquetry | Plain or small-patterned rugs or carpets Oriental rugs |

| Period Style | Associated Styles | Walls & Ceilings | Floors | Floor Coverings |
|---|---|---|---|---|
| Spanish Renaissance | Italian Renaissance<br>Early English<br>Louis XIV | Rough plaster<br>Painted<br>Ceilings same<br>or beamed | Hardwood<br>flooring<br>Tiles<br>Vinyls in tile<br>pattern | Spanish or<br>Oriental rugs |
| Early Colonial | All Early English styles<br>William & Mary<br>Queen Anne<br>wing chair | Oak panels<br>Rough plaster<br>with oak<br>Parquetry ceilings | Hardwood<br>flooring or planks<br>Vinyls in jaspe<br>pattern | Braided or hooked<br>rugs |
| Early American | Late Georgian<br>Chippendale<br>Queen Anne<br>Duncan Phyfe<br>French Provincial | Smooth plaster,<br>light trim<br>Wallpaper, scenic<br>and Chinese de-<br>signs<br>Paneling<br>Ceiling plaster | Dark hardwood<br>flooring<br>Vinyls in plain or<br>jaspe patterns | Hooked, braided,<br>Oriental, or domestic<br>rugs<br>Carpet, plain, two-<br>toned patterned |
| Modern | Swedish Modern<br>Chinese Chippen-<br>dale | Painted solid<br>colors, striped,<br>figured<br>Plain papers<br>Combinations<br>of above | Hardwood<br>flooring<br>Parquetry<br>Vinyls in modern<br>pattern | Carpet<br>Rugs in solid colors,<br>geometric patterns |
| French Provincial | 18th-century<br>American<br>Colonial<br>Federal | Smooth plaster<br>Wallpaper in<br>scenic or geo-<br>metric designs | Hardwood<br>flooring<br>Parquetry | Aubussons<br>Homespun carpet,<br>small-patterned<br>Oriental rugs |
| Victorian | Colonial<br>William & Mary<br>Queen Anne | Large-patterned<br>paper | Hardwood<br>flooring | Carpet in<br>large patterns<br>Oriental rugs |

## WINDOWS

Window design is a powerful decorating tool. It can transform an ordinary room into a setting of spectacular architectural excitement; it can "turn on" the decorative impact of your furnishings. It's the fastest and prettiest way to create visual interest, to pull together the diverse style elements of a room, and to change architectural defects into assets. Inventive window treatment challenges your imagination to come up with the right combination of curtains, draperies, blinds, shades, valances, or cornices to suit that specific window and room.

### Curtains and Draperies

Curtains and draperies are an important factor in decorating any room. Draperies date back to the earliest times, originally being used to keep out the cold. In the Middle Ages, tapestries were used, and draper-

80

ies, for purely decorative effect, date from that period. Today, draperies are also called over-draperies, over-curtains, and (colloquially) drapes.

Fabics you choose for curtains and draperies for your windows will depend upon the effect you wish to achieve. Sheer curtains covering the window, for example, will filter the light to some extent and give you a feeling of privacy in the daytime. You'll be able to see out—but others won't be able to see in.

Sheer fabrics which will serve this purpose include marquisette, ninon, voile, batiste, and lace. Marquisette and ninon are the most transparent fabrics. Batiste, voile, and lace are more opaque fabrics and shut out more of the view. Since sheer fabrics must be made from small yarns, choose fabrics containing strong fibers to obtain the best wearing qualities. Polyester is the most satisfactory fiber for marquisette and ninon fabrics. It has high strength and good resistance to the ruinous effects of sunlight and of atmospheric pollutants. Polyester blended with cotton or with rayon is frequently used in batiste and voile. This blend gives a more opaque fabric which has good wearing qualities and easy-care features. Marquisette, ninon, batiste, voile, and lace are all soft fabrics. They will look best when used as straight panels shirred on rods or pinch-pleated for use on traverse rods. They may be used alone or under draperies.

Glass fiber is used in heavier fabrics with an open-weave appearance. Glass fibers have good resistance to sunlight and atmospheric pollutants; however, these fabrics must be handled with care in laundering. Curtains and draperies containing glass fibers will have a statement on the label cautioning you about their care.

Fabrics for draperies vary from such informal types as homespun and denim to formal ones, like damask and antique satin. Heavyweight, thick fabrics will shut out all light and give privacy at night without the use of additional blinds. Lighter-weight fabrics may not give the degree of privacy desired.

Many fibers and blends of fibers are being used for drapery fabrics. Fibers which have given the most satisfaction when used alone include cotton, acrylic, and glass fibers. Blends of the following types have been satisfactory: cotton and rayon, cotton and polyester, rayon and polyester, and rayon and acetate. Cotton, acrylic, polyester, and glass fibers are more resistant to the effects of sunlight than are rayon and acetate.

The kind of care you wish to be able to use will influence your choice of fabrics for curtains and draperies. Many fabrics on the market today are machine washable. Durable-press finishes give easy-care qual-

ities to fabrics. These finishes are most satisfactory when used on blends of polyester with cotton or rayon.

Drycleaning is recommended for fabrics of 100 per cent rayon, and blends of rayon with cotton or acetate, to prevent shrinkage. Glass-fiber fabrics must always be hand washed, since machine washing or drycleaning will cause damage by abrasion in the machine.

Atmospheric pollutants as well as sunlight cause deterioration of the fibers. These pollutants are invisible and won't always be accompanied by tiny particles which cause obvious soiling of fabrics. In areas where there are high levels of pollutants more frequent washing or drycleaning will be necessary to remove the pollutants and give longer life to fabrics.

Dyes used in fabrics are not all equally fast to sunlight and atmospheric pollutants. It's difficult to predict what effect sunlight and atmospheric conditions will have on colors. Undyed fabrics or those with very light shades of color may be a better choice for curtains or draperies in areas of intense sunlight, as color change will be less noticeable. Fabric manufactured for clothing doesn't have the colorfast qualities required for curtains or draperies. Brightly printed percales may fade easily and thus give limited satisfaction.

Linings in draperies, either attached or separate, give protection against sunlight damage. Linings can

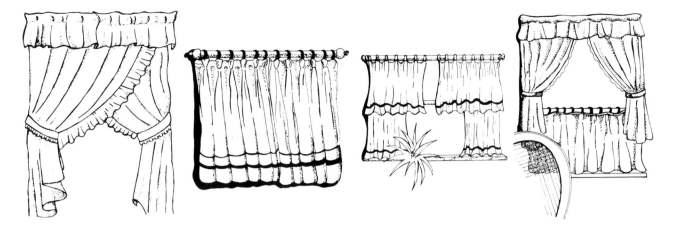

**Priscilla**          **Panel**          **Cafe**          **Cottage**

also provide more insulation and light control.

The style of window hangings you choose will determine the type of window hardware to purchase. The selection includes cafe traverse rods, adjustable traverse rods, combination traverse and valance rods, single or double curtain rods, spring-tension cafe rods, and rods that will fit around corners. Rods come in many decorator styles and colors. For special window areas, rods can be custom made or cut by stores that offer such services.

The most popular curtain styles today include:

1. *Priscilla.* These curtains are fluffy, ruffled, and feminine, and can be either floor-length or sill-length, as shown. Overlap can be partial, as shown, or complete. Tie-backs are of same ruffled materials as curtains.

2. *Tier.* Tier curtains are composed of two or more sets of overlapping short curtains. At one time, each tier ended in a ruffled flounce, but tailored tiers are now more popular than the ruffled.

3. *Panel.* Panel curtains are straight, draped curtains of floor or sill length. Each panel should run the full width of the window. One pair is illustrated. Using several curtains of this style improves effect of fullness.

4. *Cafe.* These curtains cover half the window's height and are usually simple, hemmed curtains of patterned material. Most installations use two sets per window, mounting one set above the other as illustrated. Adding a valance also helps.

5. *Cottage Set.* Cottage curtains combine straight curtains of cafe type with tie-backs, as pictured above. Tie-backs, not so popular any more because of the increased use of traverse rods, don't usually overlap.

Draperies in most home decorating arrangements are used in three principal lengths: 1) in informal rooms such as sunrooms and breakfast rooms, or in the case of small windows high above the floor, draperies can hang to the lower edge of the window apron; 2) in formal rooms, they may be long enough to permit spreading the ends on the floor; or 3) in the

vast majority of cases, the draperies should hang to the floor. All lengths can be used with or without valances.

If you want your draperies to hang in richer and more formal folds, linings will give the needed weight. Linings also give a uniform appearance to the windows from the outside. Some figured fabrics lose their decorative effect when too much light filters through. Linings are usually made from sateen in white or off-white, depending upon the background of the fabric used.

Conventional draw draperies are pinch-pleated panels which can be drawn across the glass. On a traverse rod, they let you control light and air, and provide privacy. The most popular version calls for a pair of draperies which close in the center of the window. It's a two-way draw. A variation is the one-way draw; a single fabric panel pulls in one direction across the entire window. Because the panel can draw from either right or left, one-ways sometimes seem confusing; but happily, they're not. Face the window. If you want the cords on the right and the open drapery to "stack back" on the right, the treatment is a right-to-left hand draw. If you want everything on the left, it's a left-to-right hand draw. A third version uses three or more panels of draperies simultaneously controlled by a single cord. It's a multiple draw and requires custom drapery hardware.

Double-draw draperies are just like regular draw except that there are two layers of fabrics at the window. Underdraperies, usually sheer, hang close to the glass; overdraperies, usually opaque, hang "roomside." Because there are two coverings, double draws are especially helpful in controlling the temperature of a room—without adjusting the thermostat. The sheers can be closed when the sun is very bright—letting in its light, but cutting back fading. Closed sheers also provide some privacy even when the overdraperies are open. Another reason for their popularity is that many people like the "finished" look of a soft sheer across the glass. Like regular draw draperies, double draws can be made in pairs to close in the center of the window (two-way draw), or they can be made in single panels to close one way across the glass (one-way draw).

It's important to know that draw draperies do not always have to be pinch-pleated. Modern drapery rod systems allow you to have draw draperies accordion pleated, rippled folded, or used as flat panel draperies.

Accordion-pleated draperies have an almost architectural look—one that's especially appropriate in a crisply modern room. The vertical pleats lead the eye upward and tend to "lift" the ceiling. Also, these draperies look the same from outside the house or inside the room. When open, they stack back in just about half the space needed by pinch-pleated draperies, so they're an excellent choice for glass walls or wide, wide windows. They let in a lot more light than conventional draperies, and also take less fabric.

The ripple fold, because it's soft and gentle, is more "mixable" than that of accordion pleats. But because the fabric falls in well-mannered columns, the treatment's still somewhat architectural in feeling, and so goes well in "straight-line" settings.

Flat panel draperies are similar to *shoji* sheets. In the Far East, they know that hanging fabric flat has many advantages: it's dramatic; you see every bit of its beauty; it takes much less yardage to cover any window; and it's easier to clean than fuller treatments.

Before ending the subject of drapery systems, it may be a good idea to say a word or two about the electric systems that are available to open or close them. These systems are for wide, long, or heavy draperies, or for places that are hard to reach. These electric drapery track systems can be used with conventional pinch-pleated draperies or with accordion-pleated or ripple-fold drapery heading systems.

Valances are the top or horizontal portion of the drapery treatment. They were originally used to hide the drapery poles and fixtures, but have survived for decorative reasons. Valances of light material can be shirred or ruffled, and are most frequently used in bedrooms. They are customarily 4 to 6 inches in depth for standard sized windows. When using valances of heavier materials, tailored or draped effects of varying shapes and styles are commonly used. Simpler types of valances are the most effective, although period rooms may require special treatment. Flat, shaped valances are usually lined with heavy material for stiffness. These should be from 8 to 12 inches in depth, and should never exceed one-sixth of the total window depth. Valances matching the color of the window shades can be installed on curtain rods offering pleasing mix-match combinations.

Cornices are box-like shapes sometimes used instead of valances. They are generally from 4 to 7 inches deep and made of wood or metal. Some are painted to match the woodwork or the draperies. Others are covered with the drapery material, mirrors, carved or molding designs, or with applied plaster decoration. They add to the apparent height of short windows. There are many different shapes and designs of valances and cornices. Those shown here are the most common and popular.

Window draperies can be greatly affected by the pattern of the material. The following points should be considered in making any selection of fabrics. Vertical patterns or stripes make a window appear taller and narrower. Horizontal patterns or stripes make a window seem shorter and wider. Small floral or geometric designs tend to increase the apparent size of windows. Large floral or geometric designs make a window seem smaller. Generally, large patterns are best for large rooms, small patterns for small rooms. The length of the drape should determine the scale of the pattern. Care should be taken that drapery pat-

**Accordion-pleated draperies with horizontal stripes give a strong, architectural look.**

**Sheer curtains have the double advantage of allowing light in and of providing privacy.**

terns don't clash with those in the carpet or rug.

## Window Treatments

The following suggestions are of a general nature, but may assist you in deciding on individual window treatments. Valances shouldn't be used in rooms with extremely low ceilings. A valance with curved lines makes the window appear wider, while one with square lines makes it seem narrower. For a living-room window composed of two framed panes of glass, one above the other (double-hung), straight, hanging curtains are preferable to looped-back ones. Looping back the over-draperies tends to soften a room's severity. A pair of looped-back curtains makes a window seem narrower than a single curtain tied back to give a diagonal line.

Tie-backs should be located either above or below the center of the window to avoid the appearance of cutting the window space in half. The best spot for the individual window can be found by experimentation. Usually the higher the tie-back, the taller the window appears. Ruffled sheer curtains are best when tied back. Straight, plain ones, as a rule, are never looped back. Crisscross curtains usually make a window seem wider. Straight draperies without valance or cornice tend to make windows seem taller.

Picture windows frame your view and let in lots of welcome light. Attractive from both the outside and the inside, they have become increasingly popular in various rooms throughout the home. Some are a single pane of glass. Some are made of smaller panes that don't open. In still others, one or more of the smaller panes can be used for ventilation. Because a picture window is "surrounded" by a wall, it will look cold and lonely if left untreated. It needs the softening touch of fabric. Because it's large, it's also an easy exit for the air you heat and cool; draperies can help eliminate this as they also add privacy and charm. If your picture window is "fixed" (does not open), treat it any way you like. Because it is a focal point, be sure that treatment is a part of your room—not an afterthought. If the window has panes which open, the treatment should draw away from, and stack to the side of them, as draw draperies and cafe curtains do.

A glass wall is just a "big" picture window and should be treated as such. A light-diffusing sheer draw drapery can be enough. But if fading from sunlight will be a major factor, if you'd like better control of the inside temperature, or if you just enjoy a cozy room at times, a double-draw treatment is best. Since a glass wall is a focal point by itself, it's a good idea to keep its drapery treatment simple. A lightly textured

sheer or a tone-on-tone pattern usually looks better at a wide window than a flat-weave fabric. If you want patterned draperies, keep the window's size in mind. A large design is usually in better scale than a delicate or petite one.

A sliding door consists of two glass panels—one fixed, one free to slide behind it. It may be part of a glass wall or it may be set in a solid wall, where it also serves as a large window. (Some small windows also slide—treat them the same as you would a door.) In most cases, though not all, a simple treatment is best. A sliding door is handsome in and of itself. Just remember, the treatment must never interfere with the function. Single- or double-draw draperies are best. Mount the traverse rods well above the door so that the drapery headings don't get tangled when the door is used. And be sure the draperies draw away from the opening and stack back well to each side of it.

Slanting windows are triangular affairs that follow a sloping roof line and top a glass wall. Most frequently, only the glass below is draped. The slanted top is left untreated—to provide light inside and beauty both inside and out. Almost the only time you'll want to cover the top part of a slanting window is when sunlight is a major problem. If you do cover it, use a stationary treatment. Pinch-pleated panels will coordinate with draperies on the glass wall. Or use shirred sheer curtains, preferably held on all three sides. You'll want to have any treatment for a slanted window custom made, and the drapery hardware must be cut-to-measure.

A clerestory window, like a slanting window, follows the roof line. The one truly distinguishing feature of a clerestory is that it is always set over a solid wall—not one of glass. It may be slanted but it can also be a long and shallow rectangle. Although this kind of window does give you extra wall space and a good deal of built-in privacy, it doesn't give much light and its unusual shape can bring up decorating questions. If your clerestory is slanted, it's best not to treat it at all. Remember, a slanted window treatment is a permanent covering—and you'll want all this window's light. If the clerestory is rectangular, draw draperies are fine. In most cases, you'll want to match them to the wall. This plays down the window's awkward shape. And keep them short—there's too much wall below to cover up. Because a clerestory's high, and cords may be a bit difficult to reach, consider an electric track system—controls go on the wall wherever most convenient.

An arched window curves gracefully over straight sides. It's every bit as beautiful as it is unusual. To decorate it properly, never interfere with the window's lines. Either confine your treatment completely within the window frame, or put the draperies all the way off the window so that they frame it on both sides. To "frame" this window, merely mount a standard traverse rod on the ceiling. To put draw draperies within the frame, use a standard traverse rod just below the curved part of the window—leave the top arch untreated. Or, if the sunlight is a major problem, cover the curved section with a sheer, closely fitted curtain. A third, more formal way to treat an arch is to fit stationary draperies to the curve and tie them back within the frame. This treatment—and any others which follow the curve—should be custom made.

Casement windows often require special curtain treatment. Those that swing inward are generally fitted with shirred sheer curtains fastened to the top and bottom of the windows. Those that swing out are usually fitted with straight hanging curtains or draperies. To present a uniform appearance from the street, all windows on the same floor should have the same kind of curtains or lined draperies.

Bay windows or two adjacent windows are best treated as one with a single drapery at the outer edge of each. This gives the effect of one large window and makes them appear much wider than if each window has its own pair of draperies. If a valance is used, it

**An interesting treatment which makes the window appear wider than it actually is.**

should run continuously across the windows.

Frequently found in contemporary homes, the horizontal strip window is wide and shallow. It's not ceiling high, but it is far enough above the floor that furniture can be placed against the wall below. Like the clerestory, you'll likely want all its light. When a horizontal strip window is above a work area like kitchen counters, or above a large piece of furniture like a bookcase, you'll end your treatment at the apron. But in other places, you'll probably find the window's proportions more pleasing if you make it seem deeper than it is. You can add a valance at the top over the wall. Or you can hang cafe curtains from sill to floor. Most horizontal strip windows slide open and closed. Some are made in two sections that push out. Either can wear any window treatment style—just put the rods above the frame and well out over the side walls.

A dormer window is an upper-story window tucked into a gable. Attractive from the outside, it doesn't have to be a problem on the inside. But because a dormer window tends to "tunnel" light and air, you will want to make its treatment fully functional. As for its decoration, the window and surrounding walls should be treated as a single unit. If you can build a shallow dormer out of the "real" wall level—with a desk or window seat—you'll have more freedom in

**Another very popular drapery design.**

design. If not, most people prefer to decorate the entire area in a single color and/or fabric. Small-scale patterns work, and white or just-off whites will make the most of light. Although a simple setting is usually preferred, dormer windows can be great for strong, contrasting colors, too. To help the window function well, you can use draw draperies, wall-to-wall; cafe curtains with their pretty rods and rings; or trimly tied-back curtains.

French doors are paired doors of glass—a walk-through window, if you will. Some swing in to open; some swing out. Because the area involved is large, draperies will add to beauty, provide privacy, and help control both sunlight and inside temperature. But because the door must function as a door, you'll want a treatment planned for this. If your doors open out, handle them much as you would a picture window—but no cafe curtains, please. If they open in, treat them as you would oversized in-swinging casements.

One basic rule for "door draperies" will help you handle either kind. When using draw draperies, be sure the panels pull all the way off the frame when they are open to allow the door to function freely. Any door can also wear close-fitting curtains, shirred top and bottom, held out of the way by rods placed on the door at each end.

Some entry doors are made with panes of glass. The idea is to let you look out to see who's calling. However, such a door also lets the person outside look in—and that may not be desirable. If the windows in the door are small—diminutive diamonds or rectangles—your privacy is less challenged, and you are likely to leave them bare. But if your door has

more window area, you can treat it for privacy and, at the same time, add a finished look. You'll want the treatment simple and well anchored so it won't be in the way as you open and close the door. Some form of casement treatment is best. And use the same fabric as you do for other windows in the room.

Below and over leaf is a summary of window drapery usage and period styles. This is a guide and, as with everything else in interior design, it doesn't need to be followed to the letter.

**Window Shades**

Window treatments other than curtains or draperies may be the answer to your situation. There is hardly a window of any size or shape that cannot be covered with an interesting shade. Standard shades are relatively inexpensive, can block out the light, heat, and cold, and give privacy when needed.

## Draperies

| Period Style | Fabric | Colors | Design | Upholstery Fabrics |
|---|---|---|---|---|
| Early English Tudor Jacobean Charles II | Crewel, Embroideries, Hand-blocked linen, Silk & worsted damask, Velvet, Brocade | Full-bodied crimson, green, and yellow | Large bold patterns: tree branch, fruits, flowers, oak leaf, animals, heraldic designs | Tapestry Leather Needlework Velvet Brocade |
| Anglo-Dutch William & Mary Queen Anne | Crewel, Embroideries, Hand-blocked linen, Silk & worsted damask, Velvet, Brocade, India print | Full-bodied crimson, green, and yellow | Large bold patterns: tree branch, fruits, flowers, oak leaf, animals, heraldic designs | Tapestry Leather Needlework Velvet Brocade |

| Period Style | Fabric | Colors | Design | Upholstery Fabrics |
|---|---|---|---|---|
| Early Georgian Chippendale | Crewel, Embroideries, Hand-blocked linen, Silk & worsted damask, Velvet, Brocade, India print | Full-bodied crimson, green, and yellow | Jacobean motifs Classic medallions and garlands | Tapestry Leather Needlepoint Velvet Brocade |
| Late Georgian Adam Hepplewhite Sheraton Empire Federal | Brocade, Damask, Chintz, Taffeta, Satin, Toile de Jouy | Delicate subdued hues of rose, yellow, mauve, green, and gray | Classic designs, small in scale: garlands, urns, floral, animals, etc. | Damask, Brocade, Velour, Satin, Petit point, Leather in libraries |
| Louis XIV Louis XV Louis XVI | Silk, Satin, Damask, Taffeta, Muslin, Brocade, Toile de Jouy | Delicate powder blue, oyster white, pearl, rose, pale greens, mauve, yellow | Stripes sprinkled with ribbons, flowers, medallions, lyres, and other classic motifs | Petit point, Satin, Moire, Velour, Chintz, Damask, Brocade, Tapestry |
| Spanish Renaissance | Velvet, Damask, Crewel, India print, Printed and embroidered linen | Rich vigorous colors, red, green, and gold | Bold patterns in classic and heraldic designs; also arabesques | Leather Tapestry Velvet Linen Brocatelle |
| Early Colonial | Crewel, Embroideries, Hand-blocked linen, Silk & worsted damask, Velvet, Brocade | Full-bodied crimson, green, and yellow | Large bold patterns: tree branch, fruits, flowers, oak leaf, animals, heraldic designs | Tapestry Leather Needlepoint Velvet Brocade |
| Early American | Toile de Jouy, Damask, Chintz, Organdy, Cretonne | All colors, but more subdued than in early period | Scenic Birds Animals Floral | Haircloth Mohair Linen Chintz Velours |
| Modern | Textured and novelty weaves All fabrics | All colors, bright to pastel | Solid colors Modern designs Stripes | All Fabrics Novelty weaves Plastics |
| French Provincial | Chintz Cretonne Hand-blocked linen Velvet | Subdued colors Pastel shades | Screen prints Block prints | Solid colors Textured weaves Tapestry |
| Victorian | Velvet Brocade Damask | Turkey red Other rich colors | Solid colors Formal patterns | Haircloth Needlework |

Shades can be very attractive and furnish good control of light.

87

tian blind. Needless to say, window blinds have come a long way since then.

**Venetian Blinds.** Today's so-called venetian blinds have slats that are much narrower than those of even the 1960s; in fact, slats of the ultra-slim blinds that are now so popular are only about one inch wide. Close them for a soothingly subdued light on the brightest day; open, there's little to obstruct one's view.

All designs of venetian blinds look well on windows and fit in with many color and decorative schemes. They tend to give an impression of height and width in small windows. These blinds can also be used to divide room areas, to cover open shelves where a door would be awkward, or as protection against sun glare on porches and terraces. Available in a wide range of decorator styles and colors, they become almost as much a part of the architecture as the windows themselves. By the way, they can be designed or covered with a pattern to match a wallcovering or upholstery design. Venetian blinds can be used with or without curtains or draperies.

Vertical blinds, generally made of lightweight aluminum or steel, are available in a wide variety of colors; you can create a striped or graphic effect by

Window shades are made of oiled muslin, pyroxylin-coated plastic, jute, or glass fiber. Laminated shades—cotton, rayon, or linen fabrics bonded to shade cloth—are becoming popular. They can be either translucent or transparent, for light control, or opaque for darkening effects. Shades add to the architectural grace of a house. Special types are available for almost every kind of window—picture, casement, corner, cathedral, etc. They help reduce heat loss and screen out noise. Solid-colored shades are predominantly pastel tan, green, white, and off-shades of white. Pale shades diffuse light, darker ones reduce or even eliminate it. Shades in stripes and floral patterns enhance decorative effect. Vertical stripes make windows seem taller; horizontal ones create the illusion of wider windows. Shades were traditionally pulled down from the window top, but the new "bottom-up" ones permit unusual window treatments. Consider trims, painting, applique, and stenciling for dressing up window shades.

## Blinds

According to some historians, Nero instructed his royal sculptor to create a window which would provide him with privacy, yet allow him to view his beautiful city of Rome. He designed a series of stone slabs set in a tilted fashion. *Voila,* the creation of the vene-

**Slimmer than ever, venetian blinds offer varied lighting possibilities.**

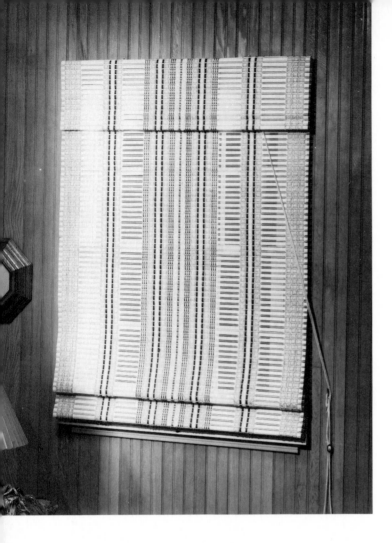

**Woven wooden blinds will give a natural look and can be used with or without additional window treatments.**

beneath cafe curtains.

Shutters may be made from wood or metal. Natural wood tones are often used to enhance the beauty of the shutters. The inside section may be made from any of the following materials: fabric mesh, cane, grill cloth, or screening. Remember that decorator colors match shutters to furnishings, and wood tones let shutters wear a natural beauty.

### Problem Windows

Problem windows are problems only as long as you believe they are. You can discover many ways in which windows can be made to look taller, shorter, wider, or thinner. Their treatment can pose an interesting challenge. You may have several windows in one wall and believe that an impossible task is at hand. Where double or triple windows are close together, it may be advisable to treat them as one window and use a single pair of draperies to cover them.

Consider using several pairs of ruffled curtains placed side by side to create an entire unit covering multiple windows and connecting wall areas. Another solution may be to use one long cafe curtain covering the lower half of the windows, and a single valance at the top.

When dealing with separated windows on a wall, alternating sections of draperies and sheer curtains may

combining several colors. Also available are rigid vertical louvers with grooves in their slats for sliding in strips of wallcoverings or fabric.

**Woven Wood Blinds.** These blinds have horizontal reeds—long slats of wood from ¼ to 1 inch in width, that are held together by decorative vertical yarns. They range in designs that are made mostly from exposed wood to those that are mainly yarns of several colors creating various interesting effects. You can use woven wood blinds with many window treatments including draperies, cafe curtains, and such shade types as Roman-fold, spring-rolls, cord and pulley, and duo-fold. Top treatments include canopies, valances, and arches, while scallops, fringes, and trims are suitable for the bottom. Because woven wood blinds add color and texture to a window, they are particularly adaptable to the "natural" look in decorating.

Woven aluminum blinds—thin aluminum strips substituted for wood slats—are available and can be used in the same manner as the wood type.

### Shutters

Inside shutters can be used next to windows in place of curtains. Some are put under curtains or draperies; others are used cafe style either above or

**Attractive use of shutters in a modern setting.**

**Unusual window treatment with an oriental flavor.**

be used to cover the entire wall. Place the draperies over the wall sections between windows. This technique will give a unified appearance to the entire area.

Any two windows that meet, or almost meet, in a corner are corner windows. They're nearly always the same height, but they may be different widths. What-

ever their dimensions they're really most attractive. Your first decision is a basic one: do you want your treatment to open and close just as it would at a picture window—two panels controlled by a single cord; or would you prefer to be able to shut out the sun at one window while leaving draperies open at the other? For the first, you'll need a cut-to-measure

traverse rod; but there are several ways of accomplishing the second. For instance, you can use two one-way draw traverse rods and butt them in the corner. Or you can use two-way draw rods butted in the corner. The principle is the same as with the one-way draw, but the draperies will close in the center of each window instead of at the sides. With this treatment, you'll always have fabric in the corner—where it can cover unattractive woodwork or a narrow strip of wall.

Other so-called "problems" and possible solutions may be one of the following:

1. *Unnecessary windows.* Cover with decorative inside shutters. Cover window with wall board and make bookcase or closet to cover. Place shelves in front of window or create a shadowbox and use as a knickknack shelf. Cover with draw curtains in bright colors.

2. *Large windows.* Cover excess portion with valance and drapes. Shorten the window with a window box.

3. *Small windows.* Hang wide drapes and curtains above and beyond the window margins, and to the floor. Create a border with wallcovering, hanging drapes outside the border.

4. *High narrow windows.* Hang curtains partly outside window frames. Treat group of windows as one with valance or cornice board.

5. *High windows on the side of a fireplace.* Place or build bookshelves under the windows. Paint them to match the woodwork or walls. Eliminate fussy drapery treatments. Block out windows with shelves or shutters. Make window a background for shelves and display colorful glassware. If you don't need the light, the window casing can be used as a frame for a picture backed with plywood.

6. *Unsightly view.* Screen it with floor-length, translucent glass-fiber curtains, so they will let in the light but keep out the view. These curtains may be finished at the bottom with weighted tape so they will stay in place. Or use shelves of glass, holding plants or colored glass vases and bowls. Venetian blinds or woven wood blinds are effective screens.

If light and privacy are needed in the breakfast or dining room, you may want to use a cafe curtain which covers the bottom of the window, and panels at the top, separated to admit light. Be innovative in your use of available materials to create the desired illusion.

When a full window treatment is not desired, you may want to have a valance at the top of your window to harmonize with the decorative scheme of your room. For a kitchen window that faces the children's play area or a wooded area where the view is important, consider a shirred ruffle hung from a regular curtain rod, or a pleated valance suspended from a cafe rod. Use your imagination to create effective treatments when a decorator's touch is needed.

The window treatment that you choose should depend on your personal taste and style of life. Factors to be kept in mind include the desired visual effect, care requirements, and environmental conditions present in your geographical location.

# THE IMPORTANCE OF accessories and lighting 5

The total-theme concept is important in creating a responsive mood; a mood in which you can feel comfortable can make a fine decorating plan. But this mood can't be captured solely by color, furniture, and wallcoverings. The completeness of a theme doesn't come across unless complemented by eye-catching, conversation-sparkling accessory objects, and motivating lighting moods.

## ACCESSORIES

How many times have you heard, "It's the little things that count?" And here it is again, on the subject of your home. Accessories are the little things—and you should consider them before and not after the fact. Much as the number of people in your family—and your current and future life styles—will help you make the right selection of furniture, so they will with accessories. If you're an inveterate reader, you'll need bookcases. If entertaining is your first love, do have a fabulous home bar to hold the "wherewithal"; but, be sure that it's decorative enough to make your room beautiful while it makes your guests happy. If you're a collector at heart, a simple glass-topped coffee table can keep elegant family silver on display. Do you enjoy the formalities of life? Then, ornate mirror frames will reflect the real you, just as a handsomely carved occasional table will say that yours is a crystal-and-champagne taste.

There are, of course, two general categories into which most accessories fall: 1) functional accessories; and 2) purely decorative accessories. The latter includes such items as paintings, photographs, wall plaques, sculptures, and most so-called "collectibles." Actually, collections of spoons, decorative china, porcelains, etc., used as accessories can be valuable assets in decorating. Frequently, a collection will be more interesting and carry more importance in the room decoration if arranged in a grouping than scattered around different portions of the room as single pieces. A collection can also serve as the starting point for an entire scheme, as the basis of a decorating focal point, or for accent colors.

The functional accessories perform a service as well as being beautiful, and include such items as clocks, cigarette boxes, ashtrays, room screens, pillows, table and floor lamps, candlesticks, and mirrors. Books, plants, flowers, copper, pewter and brass accents, elegant crystal, and decorative shelves can also be considered functional accessories. In fact, one of the most natural and effective ways to accessorize is with plants. Greenery and flower arrangements fit every home no matter what the style. Bathrooms, kitchens, living, dining and family rooms all seem to come to life, become more livable and more inviting with plants. Generally, children's rooms are the only areas where plants are not recommended.

Books are another very important accessory to any home or apartment. They can give a room a feeling of warmth quicker than any other accessory. And like plants, books give you a lot of decorating mileage for a minimal amount of money.

Another accessory that plays an important role in most rooms is pictures. In addition to the subject matter, they should be selected so that color and frame

Form an interesting wall arrangement with a collection of antique clocks.

style go with the room. While a Picasso or Dali print wouldn't look too well in an Early American home, they would be fine in a contemporary setting. Wild abstracts or expressionistic renderings likewise would not be used in ranch or traditional homes.

It's important to keep in mind that a picture isn't necessarily good because it's an original or an oil painting. Really good art is available at moderate costs in the form of good reproductions of top-quality originals. These reproductions are not "real" in the sense of originality, but they do reproduce the original faithfully. A good reproduction can capture the tangible and intangible qualities of good art. Original, signed etchings and lithographs, and good reproductions of contemporary oil and water colors are available at moderate prices from local galleries. Of course, many galleries are now featuring the works of "unknown" artists at prices anyone can afford. Actually, you can often create more interest in many cases by purchasing such original works than by buying good reproductions.

In most cases, picture frames should be simple so as not to detract from the picture. They may be natural wood, tinted, black, or colored to harmonize with the decor. Metal frames also fit into the decorating plans. Emphasis may be given to a small picture by matting. The mat may be white or tinted, 2 inches or more in width all around (slightly more at the bottom). Mat board, leather, novelty papers, fabrics, etc., may be used. The inside edge of the matting may be colored for additional emphasis. Matting also serves to allow pictures of different sizes to be framed uniformly. The extreme in framing simplicity is a small chrome base or double brace, which holds picture, mat, and glass or plastic cover, with no other frame visible.

Occasionally the frame itself is to be emphasized. Ornate gold frames, gingerbready frames, or those painted white or antiqued in a gray and gold pattern, are effective decoration.

If possible, pictures should be hung with no wire or cord showing. Usual height should be eye level. Pictures hung low add height to a room. They should be hung in groups of two, three, or more, one over the other, side by side, or in a symmetrical arrangement. Avoid stair-stepped arrangements however, except on stair walls. Pictures should harmonize with furnishings in color and style. An important picture may be the center of attraction in a room.

Mirrors can also be used effectively as accessories in any room. Frames should harmonize with decor in style. Frames may be metal or imitations of metal (as Federal), carved, plain, molded or painted wood (as Pennsylvania Dutch), painted frame glass mirrors, or mirror baguettes (either flat, shadowbox stye, or beveled out). The frame may be in any period style. They may be oval-shaped, rectangular, or shaped to fit a particular area. Mirrors set into a wall are, as described in Chapter 4, effective in adding light and size

**A comfortable chair and some flowers make a cozy foyer.**

to the room.

Accessories needn't necessarily be *new* decorator items. The popularity of the eclectic influence has spawned the rebirth of many items, long cast adrift by former owners, which have temporarily anchored themselves in secondhand and junk stores. Such antiques or, better yet, interesting near-antiques, can be effectively blended into a modern setting with devastatingly interesting results. An old Tiffany-style lamp (it needn't be a real Tiffany) in an otherwise contemporary den can singlehandedly recapture the mood of an era with which virtually everyone identifies favorably. As mentioned earlier, no need to plunge into an antique-buying spree; a single item can make a strong statement.

Accessories determine the individual pieces of furniture, and they also help to choose the period style. Serious art collectors will decorate their homes as a showcase for the jewels that glow on their walls. Their furniture and carpeting are often monochromatic in color and simple in line to offer no distraction to their dramatic possessions. Something as simple as a mass of plants in baskets from the ceiling or on the shelves of an armoire can also be the focal point in the living room; there's bound to be a color scheme that's long on green. But please don't think that the living room is the only place for collections or accessories. In the foyer, an etagere (free-standing shelves) of collectibles sets a welcoming mood to your house; in the din-

ing room, there's the modular wall system or china closet filled with treasures to make mealtime either a traditional or a contemporary pleasure. And best of all, there's the bedroom, where a long table, rather than the conventional nightstand, can be used to hold a mass of treasures for the last look before turning out the light and the first thing seen in the morning.

A house without accessories is an unfinished product—void of the personality that makes it come alive. But one of the basic rules of accessorizing—as with most other aspects of decorating—is "don't overdo it." And when accessorizing your home, overdoing is a very easy trap to fall into. Here are a few simple rules to remember when accessorizing specific rooms.

### Entry

Pictures and mirrors are the most useful accessories in this area. Mirrors, properly placed, can make an entryway larger and more interesting. Entries are also ideal for plants. They help to tie the outdoors with the indoors; the entry hall, of course, does the same thing.

### Living Room

Because of the vast amounts of open table space, bookcases, and other spots for "doo-dads," this is one room where you must guard against over-accessorizing. Be sure that the object looks right. That is, it should be of the appropriate color, the right size, and

**A free-standing mirror is always a striking addition to any bedroom.**

properly positioned. Don't clutter tables with tiny useless objects. Keep lamps tall enough to shed proper light. Leave enough surface clear so that there will be plenty of room to lay down papers, books, and other work. On large table surfaces, such as a credenza, use a few large objects rather than many small ones. On a mantel, accessories should be neither too skimpy nor overpowering, but should call attention to the wall as a whole. Use pairs for formal balance, or set off objects with one large one. The living room is a good place to combine old styles with new. In other words, a few antique accessories—an old clock, a ship's bell, or oil-lamp base—will blend nicely with modern furniture.

## Bedrooms

Mirrors, lamps and bedspreads are the major bedroom accessories. Mirrors should be considered in as many possible locations as possible—but never as a mirrored "ceiling" over the bed. Since the bedroom can be considered a personal room, it's a good place for such accessories as favorite photographs, family mementos, whimsical keepsakes, and other similar memorabilia. If a bedroom is going to be used for double duty—as a hobby room for example—stamps or coins can be used as accessories.

## Children's Bedrooms

In children's bedrooms, there are many more accessories available other than bedspreads and lamps. Tennis rackets, record jackets, pennants, travel posters, street signs, baseball mitts, and similar items are excellent wall accessories. Another good one is a bulletin board which can be used for clippings and photos of popular movie and sports stars. Space must also be provided for display of hobbies and other objects; don't scatter them around the room randomly. That is, coordinate them into an over-all theme and be very imaginative.

## Den and Study

A den or study is where one pursues one's personal or leisure-time interests—be they writing, reading, photography, or whatever. It may house memorabilia of outdoor sports in the form of a couple of game or fish trophies, or provide the wall space for the amateur photographer's gallery.

## Bathroom

Try to give this room a little glamour. Traditionally, the bathroom—except for possibilities in a powder

**(Right) The bedroom is a perfect place for favorite personal accessories.**

**(Far right) Plants and herbs always brighten up**

room—is unexciting. But, you can give it life, however, with unusual soap dishes, plenty of plants, antique bottles, or jars of bath powder or cotton balls.

## Kitchen

When accessorizing the kitchen, it must be remembered that properly selected accessories can make a kitchen, while poorly chosen ones can defeat even the most imaginative decorating scheme. A few well-selected and strategically displayed kitchen utensils and accessories help define the kitchen's style theme, and give it a professionally decorated look.

It's not good accessorizing to attempt to cover the entire countertop, nor create a cluttered look throughout the room. A few attractive, tastefully selected accessories are much more effective. It is important, though, to choose accessories that are compatible with the kitchen's style and not place them where they might interfere with kitchen tasks. Some acces-

sories are always popular. Plants, if they are live herbs, will perk up a kitchen and enhance your cooking. Flowers in an outside window box, set on a shelf, or hanging near a sunny south window, are always colorful and cheering. Cooking utensils can be decorative as well as utilitarian. Copper molds, a handsome set of cooking tools or knives, breadboards, trivets, enameled or copper pots and pans are excellent decorations. Hang them on a pegboard, over a cooking island, or on a wall. In addition, plates or mugs can be attractively displayed; a mug rack or stand puts mugs within easy reach for morning coffee or *apres*-ski cocoa. Beautiful plates should be on display, not hidden in a cupboard for occasional use. Kitchen clocks, calendars, spice or wine racks, and other functional items are also popular accessories.

## LIGHTING

As mentioned in Chapter 2, color can have an immediate impact on the viewer. While lighting does affect the way colors look, its impact is far more subtle.

Interior lighting is a very important part of all decorating—for every surface reflects some of the light it receives. Light can be absorbed and even wasted by dark surfaces, or it can be reflected by lighter surfaces and utilized as useful illumination. Re-

96

member that this reflected light will always be tinted with the color of the reflecting surface. It's this principle of reflected light that is often responsible for making the color of painted walls appear more intense than the color of a small paint chip.

Light makes colors live. In low levels of illumination, colors are grayed and lifeless; as illumination increases, they become more vibrant and alive—even pale tints and deep wood tones. Here is a simple guide of recommended reflectances for major surfaces:

|  | MINIMUM | MAXIMUM |
|---|---|---|
| **Ceilings** | | |
| Pale Color Tints | 60% | 90% |
| **Walls** | | |
| Medium Shades | 35% | 60% |
| **Floors** | | |
| Carpeting, Tiles, Woods | 15% | 35% |
| For extensive down-lighting installations | 35% | 60% |

The reflectance of these major surfaces and the amount of light they receive serve to form the background against which most seeing takes place. They are always, whether we are aware of them or not, somewhere within our field of view. As a consequence, our visual comfort, mental attitude, and emotional mood is influenced by the balance that exists between the sources of illumination, the things to be seen, and the backgrounds against which they are viewed.

Basically, there are three broad categories of lighting: 1) general area lighting; 2) task or functional lighting; and 3) mood or decorative lighting.

### General Area Lighting.

The amount of light needed for general illumination in any given room can be obtained from one source or from a combination of several. Factors to take into consideration are the size of the room and its use. The larger the room, the greater its requirements. For example, for a small bedroom of less than 125 square feet, you can create the necessary general

lighting with three 40-watt bulbs or one 100-watt bulb. For an average-sized bedroom of up to 225 square feet, you should have five 40-watt or four 50-watt bulbs. (Remember that this is for general lighting only; work areas must be considered and handled separately.)

Extending this generalization to larger rooms does not mean that a fixture accommodating more bulbs will do the job. Although this will increase the light

**Large areas often require massive lighting.**

## Recommended Lighting For Your Home (Watts)

| Room | General Area Lighting | | Local Lighting | | Remarks |
| | Bulb | Fluorescent | Bulb | Fluorescent | |
| --- | --- | --- | --- | --- | --- |
| Living, dining room · | 150 | 60-80 | 40-150 | 15-40 | For small living room |
| Bedroom | 200 | | 40-100 | | Average size |
| Bath | 100-150 | 80 | Two 60s | Two 20s | Task lights on both sides of mirror |
| Kitchen | 150-200 | 60-80 | 60 | 10 per foot of counter | Fixture over eating area or sink—150-watt bulb, 60-watt fluorescent |
| Halls, service | 75 | 32 | | | Plus low-wattage night lights |
| Stairway | 75 | 32 | | | Shielded fixtures at top and bottom controlled by three-way switch |
| Outdoor, entry and access | 40 | | | | Wall brackets aimed down |
| Hall entrance | 100 | 60 | | | |
| Outdoor, yard | 100-150 projector | | | | Controlled from garage and house |
| Laundry | Two 150s | Two 80s | | | Placed over washing and ironing areas |
| Workshop | 150 | 80 | 60 | 10 per foot of bench | Task lights aimed at machines |
| Garage | Two 100s | | | | On ceiling, center of each side of car |

level, the gain is not proportional to the number of bulbs added. The efficient way is to supplement the existing fixture with another one, or more; in short, to dispense the light sources over a larger area.

Fixtures are the number one source of general area lighting and are usually found in kitchens, dining rooms, entry halls and in luminous ceilings in bathrooms. Such lighting is generally bright and, de-

pending on the size of the room, somewhat massive. In kitchens, for instance, the trend is toward illuminated ceilings, with fluorescent tubing covered by large, often rectangular, plastic sheets.

In certain areas of the country—notably the East and Southeast—ceiling fixtures are also used in bedrooms, particularly those used for children. But, it's better not to use centralized hanging fixtures—

particularly if you have the usual eight-foot ceiling. Here, a hanging fixture is a hazard to anyone walking beneath it. And it's also a temptation to junior Tarzans and Janes. Instead, use one that is flush against the ceiling, or even recessed. This same rule applies to entry halls with dropped ceilings.

A dining room is usually lit with a chandelier of sorts. Technically, a chandelier is any overhead multi-light fixture and it can come in a number of different styles. Chandeliers are not necessarily crystal or cut glass, nor must they be ornate. A dining room should be one of the brighter rooms in the home; chandeliers should throw off a considerable amount of light. And, while they should be properly scaled and not dominate the room, they must make a secondary and complementary contribution to the decor.

Bathrooms and kitchens should always have the brightest lights; therefore you should think in terms of illuminated ceiling treatments over sinks and dressing areas. Most people spend a lot of time in front of bathroom mirrors, and unless the light is bright and bold, shadows appear on the face, causing problems with make-up application and shaving.

Since the front door is where you must first set the mood that you wish to convey throughout your home, entry-hall lighting is extremely important. Thus, if you're emphasizing an open, airy, colorful feeling, it's vital that you have a well-lit entry. But even with darker, more traditional decor, you have to think in terms of heavy wattage in the entry area. Why? Because it brings out the richness of the interior theme.

Actually, there are many different shapes, sizes, and types of light sources designed for a variety of uses. Both incandescent and fluorescent lights are used in homes. Incandescent bulbs have filaments of tungsten which give off light when heated by electric current. It is important to select a bulb of the wattage for which the fixture or lamp was designed. Too high a wattage can cause glare or present a safety hazard, while too low a wattage gives insufficient light. Some light bulbs can be switched to three different wattages to add flexibility. There are also a variety of shapes. Fluorescent lights come in many lengths, colors, and wattages. The color can be selected to enhance the interior decoration of the room in which the light will be used. Fluorescent tubes give more light per watt than do incandescent bulbs.

Structural lighting, too, is effective if properly designed and installed, but is often disappointing when done without the correct know-how. Sometimes called "architectural" or "built-in" lighting, the struc-

tural type denotes a custom installation, designed and assembled to fit a particular situation. Because structural lighting is built right into walls and ceilings, it can be designed to blend with any period decorative motif or color scheme. It can blend or conrast with its background. Since it has very little styling, structural lighting does not become dated in appearance.

There are three structural lighting techniques for walls that are easy to install and have wide application throughout the home. The most popular is the lighted *valance*. This is always used with a window to provide "nighttime sunshine." The fluorescent wall *bracket* looks a lot like a valance, but is used mainly on inside walls away from windows. Easiest to install is the *cornice*, which is mounted at the junction of wall and ceiling and can be used with or without a window.

In many cases, the structural lighting technique is used instead of a lighting fixture for general lighting. In many rooms, added fixtures will be desired to provide specific task or decorative illumination. Walls can also be lighted by recessed louvered incandescent "hi-hat" fixtures. It is best to use 75-watt R-30 or 150-watt R-40 flood lamps. These should be centered 10 inches from a solid wall or 12 inches from a window

**An example of built-in lighting.**

## Recommended Types and Sizes of Structural Lighting Installations For Residential Interiors

| Location | Floor size of room (square feet) | Minimum length of installation when used in room with ceiling fixture (feet) | Minimum length of installation when used in place of ceiling fixture | Type (or combination) of structural lighting applicable |
|---|---|---|---|---|
| Living areas (includes living room, family room, recreation rooms) | Up to 185 | | 12 | Valance, cornice, wall bracket |
| | 185—250 | | 16 | Valance, cornice, wall bracket |
| | Over 250 | | 1 foot of structural lighting for every 15 square feet of floor area | Valance, cornice, wall bracket |
| | Average | 4 | | Valance, wall bracket |
| Dining room | Average | 8 | | Cornice, cove |
| | Average | 3 | | Valance, wall bracket |
| Dinette | Average | 3 | | Valance, wall bracket |
| Dinette | Average | 6 | | Cornice, cove |
| Bedroom | Up to 125 | 3 | 6 | Valance, cornice, wall bracket |
| | 125—225 | 4 | 8 | Valance, cornice, wall bracket |
| | Over 225 | | 16 | Valance, cornice, wall bracket |
| Vestibule | 40—80 | | 6 | Wall bracket |
| Foyer | 40—80 | | 8 | Cornice |

wall. One fixture is used for every 32 inches of wall length.

Another special structural technique is cove lighting, which is particularly well-suited to rooms with two ceiling levels. In these applications, the lighting should be placed right at the line where a flat low-ceilinged area breaks away to a higher-ceilinged space. The upward light emphasizes the change of level and is very effective in rooms with slanted or cathedral-type ceilings; but the lighting efficiency of coves is low in comparison with that of valances and wall brackets.

**Task Lighting.**

Sometimes called "local" or "work" lighting, this type of lighting is for visual jobs such as reading, sewing, playing the piano, etc. Generally it is provided by portable lamps placed close to the user, or by fixtures. When possible, task or functional lighting should contribute to the general area lighting.

Portable lamps are the most popular types of task lighting. Choose a table lamp with a minimum capacity of 100 watts; 150 watts would be better. Table lamps used for prolonged periods and floor lamps need 200 or 300 watts. This wattage is in addition to

**Here, additional lighting brings out the elegant chinaware in a built-in area.**

other sources of light in the room. The bulb should be low in the shade so the light strikes the task. Select a table lamp of good proportion. The size of the lamp should be in relation to the table and chair where it will be used, as the bottom of the lamp shade should be about level with the eyes of a person seated in the chair. Select lamps or fixtures that produce "soft" or diffused light to eliminate glare and contrasts, which cause distraction and difficulty in seeing. This is not to imply that "hard" or bright light does not have a place in lighting your home, but it should not be used as a primary source of light. The effects of various artificial light on color is covered in Chapter 2.

Select a lamp shade that blends with the background and transmits some light through the sides. Usually, light-colored translucent shades are preferred, because opaque shades create spots of uncomfortably high brightness above and below the rim of shade. Too-thin shades show "hot spots" that are distracting. Avoid narrow, deep shades, or those which are too shallow. If there is a lining, be sure it's white.

The number of lamps you need for any one room depends on its size and the amount of space to be illuminated. But the absolute minimum for a living room should be three—one at each end of a sofa and the third on a parsons table, a desk, or in an etagere.

There are other basic guidelines in working with lamps:

1. Table lamps play a practical and an aesthetic role. Their style can enhance the home decor while the color of their shades and/or base can be used as accents for your basic color scheme. In a contemporary home, clear or smoke glass or chrome-based lamps complement the clean, uncluttered, modern look.

2. When selecting table lamps, make sure they are not too big in relation to the size of the table. Even though a lamp's primary job is to illuminate the surrounding area, it should not be overpowering.

3. A dark room with paneling and earth-tone colors absorbs light while bright colors reflect and intensify light. Keep that in mind when placing fixtures and lamps.

4. A small room can be well lit by only a couple of lamps. Use light-colored shades through which light rays can penetrate, rather than dark shades that direct light only up and/or down.

5. If you use a desk in a room setting, always place a lamp of some kind on it.

6. Lighting can emphasize built-ins and accessories. A bookcase, for example, can be highlighted by a small fixture that fits comfortably on one of the shelves.

7. Where you have limited space, but need illumination, consider a stick table lamp. Lamp and table are a single unit, usually small in scale. These go rather well in the retreat area of a master bedroom or in a nursery next to a rocking chair.

8. In the master bedroom always use two lamps on matching nightstands. Thus each person can control a light for reading.

9. Lamps, appropriately placed, are extremely effective in creating the right mood in a den; for in-

**A good floor lamp next to a comfortable arm chair is an aid to reading.**

**Recommended Mounting Heights and Lamps for Structural Lighting in Specific Task Areas**

| Location | Mounting height | Recommended delux warm white fluorescent lamps |
|----------|----------------|-----------------------------------------------|
| Single bed | 52 inches from floor | 30-watt lamp* |
| Double bed | 52 inches from floor | 40-watt lamp* |
| Extra-wide bed or twin beds with single headboard | 52 inches from floor | Two 30-watt lamps* |
| Lounge furniture | 55 inches or more from floor | Choose lamp sizes to harmonize with length of furniture |
| Buffets | 60 inches from floor+ | 30-watt* lamp |
| Desk | 15-18 inches from desk top | 30-watt or 40-watt lamp* depending on length of desk |
| Mirror or picture grouping | Mount directly at top edge of mirror or above picture grouping | Choose lamp size to harmonize with length of furniture |

*30-watt lamps are 36 inches long; 40-watt lamps are 48 inches long.
+Less if top wall bracket is closed.

stance, a couple of lamps with dark shades create a soft, inviting atmosphere that seems to say "come on, sit down and relax and forget your worries." The den should be a study in softness and casual informality.

Don't forget that lamps are not the only way to provide lighting, even task lighting. Consider other ways: hanging pendants, down lights, wall washers, valances, coves, or wall brackets, to name a few.

Actually, spotlighting is one of the more popular types of local lighting. Some spotlights are flush mounted and set into a ceiling. Others may be fastened on a ceiling or wall with screws. So-called pinup lamps may be hung on a wall with a picture hook. Many free-standing lamps, both floor and table models, are spotlights, and may or may not have flexible goosenecks or swivels to permit the direction in which their light is aimed to be changed at will. But while every house needs spotlighting, and has many places where this technique will be a big help, spotlights may hinder more than they help, unless used carefully. Because their light is so concentrated, any object placed in the beam will cast a very strong shadow. However, this may be avoided by observing any of these precautions:

1. Place the spotlight fixture so that its light reaches the work surface directly.

2. Use more than one spotlight for a given area. When multiple lamps are used in this way, the beam from each tends to reduce the shadows cast by the others.

**(Top) In a bathroom, bright lights are needed above sinks and mirrors for applying make-up and for shaving. (Bottom) Three types of lighting, each appropriate for its particular area.**

102

**Mood Lighting.**

Artful use of accent or mood lighting can be an element of the decoration by emphasizing an art object, a picture, a planter, a brick wall, or a mural. This accent lighting adds a touch of glamour and beauty to the room and contributes to the over-all amount of light. Actually, for special effects, such as lighting a wall of pictures or an area of accessories, track lighting and ceiling-mounted spotlights are increasingly popular. Track lights, which can provide direct or indirect beams, are exceedingly compatible with contemporary furnishings. In fact, track lighting offers complete decorating freedom, providing endless opportunities to achieve functional and accent lighting. Track lighting is a concept of accent lighting that can be as flexible as the imagination. It can be recessed, surface-mounted, or suspended by pendant stems. Most of these movable, adjustable track systems can be swiveled, angled, and pointed in any direction, or grouped for every functional design effect.

**In the background, accent lighting that illuminates better and draws attention to a large painting.**

# LIVING
# rooms

6

To what extent, and in what manner is your living room lived in? It's necessary to ask this, because the function of this particular room varies widely from family to family. Some households retain the equivalent of what was once the "parlor"—a place for solemn occasions and polite conversation. In these circumstances, what was formerly the "back parlor" is now the family room, chiefly devoted to television, while in some sections of the country, or in small apartments, living room, dining room, and kitchen flow into each other, separated not so much by walls or divisions as by how each area is furnished.

Provided you've the space, a parlor-type living room is delightful. The word parlor suggests the Victorian era, and for anyone who likes a nostalgic atmosphere this is still the easiest period to simulate, besides being the most amusing if done a bit tongue-in-cheek. A more serious version of the front parlor should probably be called a drawing room. But here real quality is essential and professional help is advised, especially since many of the materials required to do a French or English drawing room well—the fabrics and the wallpaper—might have to be bought through a decorator.

However, in most homes and apartments, the living room will be the focal point of family relaxation and activity. It will also serve as the area of the home for entertaining guests, and therefore will be the main standard by which your visitors will judge your style and tastes. Occasionally there will be another area of the house that can be used as a family room, and thus be used for your family's wide array of activities. If this

is the case, you may wish to have your living room remain somewhat formal and with a touch of elegance. Naturally, if you do not have a family room, your living room will have to serve both purposes.

As is the case with other areas of the home, the living room is functional and, although it is not mandatory, should contain furniture and pieces which lend themselves to fulfilling whatever purpose for which

**A parlor-type living room.**

the living room is being used. Usually, the living room will be used for conversation, relaxation, and entertainment. The average living room will contain a sofa, two chairs, one or two end tables, and a coffee table, because they promote comfort and relaxation while serving both the needs of the family and guests. Again, the living room usually reflects the life style of the family, so there are no specific requirements on furnishings.

Furniture and its arrangement plays the largest part in adapting the living room to different occasions. Comfortable upholstered pieces supplemented by lightweight "pull-up" chairs, tables that become buffets or split up into snack tables—all are wise choices for a room which one evening may be the scene of a quiet family gathering, and the next harbor a super-scale party. Whether the room is large or small, regularly or awkwardly shaped, two or more conversation groupings—which can merge into one large group if the occasion warrants—are the starting point of the furniture arrangement. A sofa might be the pivot of the main grouping—and a love seat or pair of upholstered chairs might serve as an auxiliary, with small tables strategically placed to provide resting places for coffee cups and ashtrays.

Small living rooms may accommodate only two or three groups. Larger living rooms may have room for one large grouping and several smaller ones. Once these chords, or groups, are established, fitting them into a room is comparatively simple. Before deciding

where they go, however, mark all doors on the floor plan—traffic lanes must be kept clear. Indicate architectural centers of interest. If there is a fireplace or an important window, the major grouping should balance it or center on it from what is called an axis or center pole. The lesser groups will drop in around it.

Since the living room will be serving as that area of the home for entertaining visitors, it offers you the opportunity to experiment with unusual pieces of furniture primarily for ornamental purposes. For example, etageres, which resemble narrow bookcases, add to almost any decorating style. They are available in a variety of styles and finishes and are excellent for use as a showcase for figurines or other items that will attract attention and create conversation.

There are other odd pieces of furniture which can find use in the living room. You might consider an antique secretary or an armoire (large chests formerly used as free-standing wardrobes). These can add charm to your living room and spark interest as well, but even more importantly, they add that personal touch which helps make your living room unique.

As a general rule, begin the living room arrangement with your largest pieces of furniture, placing them against or at right angles to the longest walls. If you're short on wall space, try that sofa in front of a group of windows, thus relinquishing wall area for such a piece as a secretary, which requires wall backing. The grand piano will take less room and fit into the scheme of things best if its straight side lines up

The lush plants and unique addition of a statue create a special garden effect in this living room.

with one of the walls. Try the spinet away from the wall, if you need space. Stand it right out in the room backed by the sofa. A small chair, or chair and table, will fit into the curved side of the grand piano and helps relate this piece to the room. By looking at your completed floor plan, you'll be able to tell at a glance where you can best repeat colors and patterns. But allow space for people in your plans. Try to arrange your main conversation grouping to seat six people within eight feet of each other, for comfortable conversation. Allow a minimum of 15 inches of leg room between a sofa or chair and the coffee table.

Every living room has its own special problems which do not seem to be covered by general rules. Though it is obviously impossible to foresee and solve all of them, here are a few suggestions which may be helpful:

A *long, narrow room* is a problem area. Widen the long, narrow room with lines drawn emphatically across the room rather than with those running the long way. Do this by placing a desk, love seat, or chair grouping at right angles to one of the long walls. Much can be done to modify the proportions of a long, narrow room by a clever use of color. If you can't do this by altering the wall colors, then add bright notes in your furniture at the far ends of the room, bringing those walls closer to the center of the room and squaring them off. A mirror or a picture with a view such as a landscape or seascape, placed on the long walls and not at the ends, has a widening effect in the desired direction. Avoid rugs or carpets with the pattern running the length of the room. A horizontal emphasis, such as a sofa grouping, deliberately placed across the end of the room, also has a widening effect.

An *off-center fireplace*, with a front door opening directly to the outside, complicates a balanced arrangement, but it can be overcome by centering the main furniture grouping around the fireplace. Place a

sofa and a lamp table at right angles to the fireplace. On the other side of the fireplace, arrange a pair of chairs and lamp table. If the room is a modern open plan, a curved sofa in unit sections can come out at right angles to the fireplace and curve around the front area of the fireplace, with a large round coffee table in the center.

The *corner fireplace* is always difficult, particularly if it's not in a large room. Don't place the sofa across the front of the hearth, cutting the room in half diagonally. Keep your sofa and large pieces away and back against one of the walls, and feature a bench or small grouping at the fireplace. This arrangement doesn't interrupt the room so noticeably, yet still makes use of the fireplace.

A *fireplace between two doorways* is a particularly difficult problem, especially if traffic must pass directly in front of the chimney space. This makes it impossible to include it in any one of the major groupings of the room. In this instance, you have to divorce your major grouping from the hearth, establishing it on the wall opposite, or wherever the floor plan requires.

A *wide or center archway* directly opposite the fireplace cuts the wall space to disadvantage. Even so, don't place the sofa across the corner. Keep it "offside" in relation to the fireplace by placing it against the wall at either side of the archway; or have it at the end of the room. Better still, if your room is suffi-

The main furniture grouping is placed around an off-center fireplace.

ciently wide, you can include it in your main grouping at right angles to the fireplace.

For a small room with *no fireplace,* but a window with a view, try a pair of love seats or a pair of large armless chairs flanking the window, and place a low table between. This will form a pleasant conversational grouping which doesn't interfere with traffic through the room.

When a room has a *double traffic lane,* the solution is to arrange the room so that traffic must go around the main conversational grouping and not pass through it.

No matter what rooms you have in your home, living room, family room, den, and so on, the principles enumerated can always be applied. At the risk of being redundant, remember that before planning any of these rooms, you must know what activity is going on in the room, then plan the furnishings accordingly. The room must not only be unified and have charm, but must also be practically arranged for traffic and for everyday use. If a living room must serve more than one purpose, it should be frankly eclectic or else boldly contemporary, since neither of these ideas insists on subtle proportions or "correct" scale.

"Illusion" may be just what you need for rearranging your belongings and giving them a new background. In addition to the decorating tricks mentioned in Chapters 3 and 4, consider placing a large grouping of furniture—such as a table with a sofa on the other side of it—at the entrance to your living room, so it's the first thing seen. This would act as a foreground, and the rest of the furniture would appear farther away and, by comparison, smaller in a larger area. Other tricks are to place interesting objects in corners where the eye will go to them, and to place a long sofa on a short wall to make a room seem wider. These illusions work well in any setting, but they are particularly useful when a living room is small and you want to depart from the conventions.

There are several important factors to consider when decorating a living room. Walls, for instance, are major areas. They can be one solid color or a combination of many, and, of course the choice is left up to individual tastes as to whether paint or wallpaper is used.

To give walls a little life, try picture groups and wooden clocks in traditional homes, or chrome-framed paintings and posters for contemporary-designed living rooms. Mirrors are also excellent for setting off the walls in the living room, but be careful where you place them. Too many mirrors can make your guests uneasy, especially if they are placed directly opposite the conversation area.

Another way of adding warmth to the living room is your choice of textures and fabrics. Woven linens and suedes give a natural effect and are excellent backgrounds for soft items or figurines on open table space to break up some of the emptiness of the room. Of course, use whatever you wish, but remember, too many accessories and knickknacks tend to make your living room look too cluttered. Next, focus your attention on greenery. Plants, preferably live, blend well with whatever theme or style of room you choose. For a detailed discussion of the use of accessories, see Chapter 5.

The trend today is toward a living room that is comfortable, yet somewhat formal. It will be the place for the family to relax, but it will also be where you will be entertaining your guests. The goal in decorating the living room is to create a warm and inviting atmosphere that will be able to perform both duties.

# DINING ROOMS AND areas

**7**

While the trend toward casual and informal living has grown stronger in America, the use of formal dining rooms still persists. Convenience foods and kitchen dining facilities have become popular, but the formal dining room, especially during holiday seasons, represents family togetherness. In our grandparents' day there was never any question about the dining room. It was there. It was the room where the entire family gathered at least twice a day to take their meals in comfort and elegance. Today, to use a dining room or not is the question. One may prefer to cook in a gregarious, cozy, open-kitchen-type arrangement where good conversation goes on during the cooking. However, eating itself should be more special and more separate. In some instances, space dictates the dining corner or alcove. But the separate dining room, away from the general living area, has many advantages—not the least of which is the benefit to children. In general, manners are learned at the table. Food worth cooking is worth being enjoyed. The dining room is where the family shows off. It is the room where a family extends the essence of its hospitality and sociability, whether it's a formal sit-down supper or a romantic candlelit dinner for husband and wife.

The separate, formal dining room began to disappear during the Depression, along with the full-time cook and maid; and by World War II it was considered superfluous. In the mid-1960s, however, it started making a comeback, and today the separate dining room is back with us.

Of course, almost every family wants a dining room,

**The separate dining room is an elegant addition to any home.**

set apart and dedicated to the delights of good food and good company. As a separate room, it has an elegance, a sense of leisure not associated with dining areas included in family room or kitchen. However, elegance does not necessarily mean rigid, stately formality. The classic symmetry of a table surrounded by chairs, basic to most dining rooms, may be the only formal touch. Whether the room is formal or informal depends on the style of table, chairs, and auxiliary

108

pieces, their arrangement, the color scheme, and the materials selected to cover background expanses. When deciding on your decorative scheme, think of your dining room as the setting for every kind of meal you like to serve to guests and family—from buffet luncheon to formal dinner, from French *haute cuisine* to fondue cooked at the table. With the broadening of today's dining and entertaining horizons, dining-room versatility is an asset, if not a necessity. Subtle decorative treatment is a key to the room's comfortableness and adaptability.

**Dining-Room Furniture and Arrangements**

Conventional dining-room furniture is frequently purchased as a suite: a table; four, six, eight or a dozen chairs; a buffet; a china closet; or a serving table. A breakfront may replace a buffet, and in smaller rooms the china closet may be omitted entirely. If you have imagination and will, however, endless furniture variations and combinations are possible. But, since there is seldom an alternative to having a table and chairs in the center of the room, decorating a dining room can present a challenge to one's ingenuity. Unless you plan some really interesting decorative innovations, you can fall into the trap of having a dining room that seems dull and ordinary. There are three main avenues of escape from mo-

notony—furniture, backgrounds, and accessories.

The more flexible you are in your choice of furniture, the less stereotyped will be the final effect. Just as most people are no longer choosing the matched three-piece suite of sofa and two chairs for the living room, or the tiresome bed-dresser-chest suite for the bedroom, they are learning to mix rather than match in the dining room. In less formal rooms try Welsh dressers, cupboards with hutch tops, corner cupboards, old washstands, brass French bakery racks, tilt-top tables, grandfather clocks, a stack of Korean chests; even a highboy may offer drama, as well as storage space, and take the place of more conventional pieces.

You can mix styles, finishes, colors, and woods—anything as long as the end result is harmonious. Chairs, for example, need not match the table, nor need they match each other. It's far more interesting to see a pair of unusual host and hostess chairs teamed with four side chairs in another style. An antique hutch picked up at auction, an old desk or breakfront rescued from the attic, or a new tea cart with lacquered finish—any of these might blend in beautifully with the rest of your dining room furniture. If you already own a matched set and your room needs more contrast, try painting the chairs and table in a

If the size of the room permits, additional furniture such as this china cabinet and breakfront provide variety as well as cupboard space.

color that sets off the wood tones of the buffet and other cabinets.

Sometimes a dining room is too small to permit much leeway in mixing furniture. In this case, a wall of built-in shelves and cabinets would be an interesting addition. Generally, however, oak, walnut, maple, cherry, and painted pieces hobnob pleasantly in Early American or country dining rooms. Satinwood, mahogany, fruitwood, and walnut tables and chairs will bow graciously to each other under the glitter of a crystal chandelier.

It is usually a good idea to assemble the maximum number of chairs a dining table will accommodate. If they are rarely used together, the extra chairs serve nicely in other parts of the house—to flank a console in the hall, in the bedrooms, or at a desk in the living room. All the chairs may be armless, or you may have two host's chairs with arms. Only in very large rooms is it possible to accommodate armchairs at all places at the table. If the chairs have slipseats, they can easily be reupholstered. The change in cover and color is pleasant, and in a young family where spills occur, such changes are often necessary. In dining rooms that are contemporary or eclectic, a glass-topped table will work wonders in opening up a small area.

## Backgrounds for Dining Rooms

Decoratively speaking, it's the background of a room, rather than the furniture, that holds the most promise for creative accomplishment. The average dining room cries out for background interest, and

there are dozens of ways of doing things with floors, ceilings, and walls that will lift any room out of the ordinary.

If your dining room is small and must therefore be sparsely furnished, a floor covering can contribute some of the decorative excitement missing elsewhere. Choose a small-in-scale, but texturally interesting and colorful pattern, or any of the small-figured textured carpet patterns in muted tones of a single color. Small rugs on wood floors also furnish an interesting background.

For the architectural interest that adds so much warmth and intimacy to dining at home, look to the walls. Few recently built homes boast built-in cupboards, niches, fireplaces, paneled insets, and moldings, but such assets can be added at surprisingly small cost.

One of the easiest methods for introducing background interest is the making of a dado from chair rail molding—a simple, inexpensive molding strip available by the foot at lumber yards. When nailed to walls at a level approximating the height of the average side chair, the molding divides the wall so that upper and lower parts can be decorated differently. Usually, one part is covered with wallpaper or fabric, and the rest painted or paneled.

Scenic wallpaper, also frequently used with a wood molding so that it covers only the upper part of one wall, works best where you have the dual intent of making a room look more spacious as well as more attractive. A scenic paper brings unity to a room when it is keyed to a decorating theme—a pastoral scene for French Provincial, a New England street for Early American, a Japanese garden for Oriental moods.

Even an entranceway or an ordinary flush door might be the means of lifting a room above the mundane. To give a door an expensive look, add moldings in French Provincial, Mediterranean, or traditional feeling. As a finish, use a dark wood stain, or antique the molding in a suitable color to go with a painted

door. Painted moldings are usually teamed with French furniture, while wood stains blend better with Colonial or Mediterranean styles.

As with other rooms in the house, the use of mirrors is an attractive addition to a dining room. Mirroring is an excellent way to increase the size of the dining room visually, in addition to reflecting a decorative treatment on the opposite wall. However, it is seldom wise to use a wall of mirrors since they, in effect, double the room size and the entire room will then seem out of proportion.

For a combination of architectural interest and an aura of pleasant, old-fashioned warmth, the use of wood beams on the ceiling is most effective. Although borrowed from the past, the geometric patterns that can be formed with beams makes them compatible with contemporary decor as well. It is not necessary to have a cathedral ceiling to use them. They can be scaled down in size and kept simple in arrangement to suit a room of average proportions. Beams laid parallel to each other look well in medium-sized areas, while crossed patterns are best for larger rooms. Boxed beams can be purchased ready-made and installed by a carpenter. You may have them stained as is, but for a more rustic, old barn look, they should be given a so-called "distressed" finish.

A well-decorated window can add immeasurably to the feeling of coziness and intimacy so important to a dining room. Whether you have a picture window, bay window, French doors, casements, or the conventional double-hung type, a window can be as outstanding as you want to make it. But more often than not, meals served at the dining room table will take place after dusk, so that what your window treatment does for the room within, and how well it succeeds in affording privacy in a non-secluded area, is just as important as capitalizing on a view.

When your table is set in front of a large window, the natural tendency is for diners to indulge in occasional window-gazing as they would in a restaurant in

a picturesque setting. If there is something worth seeing both night and day, you might want sheer curtains or window shades that can be pulled up or down as needed. For emphasis, "frame" the view as you would a picture with side draperies or an upholstered padding around the window frame. To admit a view when needed and attain privacy at other times, you could combine sheer curtains with draperies on a traverse rod, or use shutters that fold back. Where there is no view at all and the very size and placement of the window seem to promise one, try creating your own scene indoors with towering plants. It's almost like dining in a garden.

To create a friendly atmosphere between family members and guests, exclude the world completely by minimizing the windows. This can be done with curtains that match the color of the wall, or window shades made from the same fabric or wallpaper that surrounds them.

### Dining-Room Accessories

Accessorizing a dining room is somewhat in a class by itself, for it is the small objects in everyday use—flatware, china, glass, and linens—that make up a large part of the room's color scheme and help determine its decorative style.

The desire to have your home look its best is stronger than ever when guests are invited to dinner. Since the table is usually set in advance, the visitor's first impression will depend on how well the total

**The use of placemats or type of tablecloth can also affect the air of formality or informality you wish to create.**

look of your decorating scheme comes off, hence, the necessity for considering table appointments as part of your over-all decorating plans. Advocates of contemporary furniture design tend to favor utter simplicity in china, glass, and silver, as a foil for exotic or vividly colorful linens, candles, and centerpieces. Those with Provincial or traditional furnishings usually have a taste for patterned tableware against conservative linen cloths.

When selecting table accessories, consider how they will look with each other as well as against the background of the room. China, silver, and glass blend best when a balance is achieved between ornateness and simplicity. If you start with heavily decorated china, coordinate it with less ornate silver and glass, or the effect will be overpowering. Don't go overboard with matching—it is the feeling of the design that should be repeated. If there are roses in the dining room wallpaper, it is all right to repeat them in china, but it would be monotonous to have rose-patterned silver and roses etched on glasses also.

Bear in mind that too much ornamentation in the more permanent accessories limits the number of ways you can vary table settings with linens, centerpieces, flower arrangements, and candelabras. Linens alone can add much to the color scheme of a room. Depending on the formality or informality of the occasion, you can run the gamut from white or pastel cloths and napkins, to placemats and runners in vivid colors and patterns. In fabrics, try to include varied patterns and textures—pastel embroidered organdies, white lace over a brightly colored background cloth, gay stripes, madras, or other plaids. Occasionally, produce the unexpected—a length of dress or upholstery fabric made into an exotic tablecloth, or a conventional tablecloth made unique with a border of ball fringe, piping, or other trim.

Keeping in step with the seasons is of special significance in the dining room, where our patterns of eating as well as living change according to the calendar. It isn't enough to switch from the hearty cold-weather fare to summer salads and iced tea if the room itself is still in the winter doldrums. By adding or subtracting a few accessories, you can key a dining room to seasonal variations.

Decorating enthusiasts live for the first days of fall, when the abundant colors of nature can be brought indoors. There are few table or sideboard decorations more attractive than a bowl brimming with fruits and vegetables of the autumn harvest. There is also much to be done with pine cones, leaves, branches, or whatever a ride into the country in your particular

habitat might yield. When the first days of winter arrive, it is time for some holiday cheer to compensate for the bleakness outdoors—tableclothes or placemats of red felt trimmed with holly leaves, poinsettias on the buffet, and lots of candles. By spring, a lighter touch is in order—hanging straw baskets of fresh spring flowers, pastel linens, and crisp white curtains. In summer, the fewer accessories the better. Anything that is heavy in scale or warm in color should be banished until fall, for a simple uncluttered background is essential to the enjoyment of light summer meals.

**Dining Without a Dining Room**

There is no questioning the fact that a dining room is nice to have, but neither is there any reason why you can't live happily without one. If you have chosen a family room as an alternative, there is really no problem, since here you can incorporate all the facilities you need for both daily meals and special occasions. When your small house or apartment yields only a kitchen or dinette space, however, a little more ingenuity is called for.

Families without dining rooms have developed a wide variety of dining techniques. They dine while seated at a dining table in the living room or foyer. They lounge in front of the television set with a tray, or enjoy a buffet supper with the aid of nesting or stacking tables. They even sit on the floor Japanese-style, in front of a low cocktail table. At small parties, guests often gather around a chafing dish on a table and cook their own Swiss fondue. Some of these possibilities are so appealing that even those who have dining rooms often join in the fun of dining elsewhere.

In order to dine as comfortably as possible despite limitations on space and the need for putting other functions first, it is essential to have the right furniture—as few pieces as possible, carefully chosen to save space, and preferably to serve more than one

function. The basics essential to dining are few—a table, chairs, and a place to store table appointments.

The range of tables available is so varied that it is possible to find a solution for almost any problem you might have. Consider these possibilities:

**The "high-low" cocktail table.** For those who insist they cannot find space for another table, regardless of its size, there are tables on swivel bases that raise up from cocktail to dining height. Place a high-low table in front of a sofa-and-chair arrangement, have extra pull-up chairs handy if needed, and your seating arrangement is complete.

**The extension table.** For dinettes, L-shaped living rooms, and foyers, various types of extensions enable you to keep the table within limited bounds when it is not in use. The dinette or foyer, for example, may be just large enough for four. When six, or eight, or even ten must be seated, you can extend the table into the adjoining living room, adding a set of folding bridge chairs or other seating. In addition to drop-leaf designs, there are tables with extensions that pull out from underneath, leaves to be inserted in the center, or the console—a hinged table that folds in half.

**The wall-hung table.** Dining tables are often incorporated into multi-functional wall arrangements. Although four at most can be accommodated, and preferably two, the wall-hung table has proved a boon to small-apartment dwellers, or even home-

owners who want a secondary dining area.

**Folding tables.** For buffet parties and occasional large groups, the strictly utilitarian folding aluminum table that can be stored in a closet is inexpensive and often indispensable. A tablecloth masks its unattractive appearance.

With so many space-saving tables available, anyone with enough open floor space in the living room can set up a table for four, six, eight, or even more. But seating a lot of people and serving them a full-course dinner in the living room takes a bit of doing.

Providing enough chairs in the non-dining room is something of a problem. For the separate dinette, dining "L," or large living room with a dining area at one end, four chairs are usually the right amount, plus two more that can be kept in another part of the living room if you select a compatible style. There are also tables intended for use in living rooms, family rooms, and indoor-outdoor areas, that come with a set of four stools stored underneath. This is fine for occasional use, but tiring as a daily routine.

For storage, you should have a place to show off your nicest things as well as keep them separate from everyday table accessories used in the kitchen. Since dinette tables and chairs are usually small, you will have to avoid overpowering them with large, tall cabinets in the small dinette or dining "L"—even though you would like to have the extra drawer and

**The breakfront is appropriate in a more spacious dining room.**

cupboard space of a large unit. Try choosing a buffet or buffet-hutch combination of modest proportions; then hang some of your pretty things from shelves or racks on the remaining walls. Or make the most of what space you have by relying entirely on built-in shelves and cabinets. If necessary, keep your china in a kitchen cabinet set aside for this purpose and find space in the linen closet for tablecloths.

When your dining area is part of a large living room, a commodious breakfront is usually functional and can prove to be the decorative focal point of the room, its size serving to balance your main seating group, which is usually at the opposite end of the room. A wall of built-ins in the living room—housing television, phonograph, bar cabinet, bookshelves, and other paraphernalia—can be planned to accommodate your china, glass, and silver as well.

When decorating a dining "L"—which amounts to a dining room just around the corner from the living room—the two areas can be decorated quite differently, as regards both the type of furniture and the wallcovering. But it must constantly be remembered that even here, as in all adjacent areas visible from each other, the colors should be related from one area to the next, although the change in pattern and texture can be as abrupt as you wish. Within any

**The wallpaper and curtains here combine nicely with the chairs' upholstery.**

open-plan, see-through interior, the decision as to where one "room" ends and another begins is entirely up to you. We don't believe you should call attention to the fact that a living-room divan can double for a bed by putting bedroom roses behind it; but otherwise, any plausible division of a wall is justified.

For example, in a small apartment the "dining room" may consist of nothing but a table and some chairs. Should you attempt to enclose them by screens or bead curtains? If you do, you may make an already small room seem smaller. Rather than cut up your floor space it might be wise to define the different areas by means of well-chosen wallcoverings, as suggested in the previous chapter. It would be sad not to point up a dining area in some way. The evening meal in particular should be heightened by romantic lighting and a colorful background. This can be provided in almost any corner of the room; the nearer the kitchen—which may merely be a closet, behind folding doors—the better.

**Here, the dining area is set apart effectively by the shelves which at the same time create a partition and an entrance-way.**

# kitchens

**8**

In planning a kitchen decorative scheme, select the style before selecting colors and materials. Keep the style of the kitchen consistent with the architectural style of the house or apartment—it takes some thought to successfully mix styles, especially in smaller living units. But today, there is no one style for a kitchen.

The charm of Early American, French Provincial, or Mediterranean design can go a long way toward making the hours spent in the kitchen a time of pleasure rather than routine drudgery. A kitchen done in contemporary style can also be cheerful and lively when a bit of thought is given to side-stepping the commonplace. Bright and cheerful color schemes and fresh, original decorating touches are doubly appreciated for the lift they give to the homemaker's spirit.

These are some of the most popular styles in kitchens, and some ideas on how to use them to best advantage.

**Early American.** Provincial cabinets in a pine or cherry finish and a pine table with ladder-backed, Windsor, Hitchcock, or captain's chairs are the basics. You might also use deacon's benches or trestle benches instead of chairs. A painted occasional piece is fresh and colorful—ladder-backed chairs in blue or yellow; black-lacquered Hitchcock chairs with stenciled backs; or a painted and decorated cupboard. Delft tile or provincial print wallpapers—Revolutionary War documentaries, or small-figured, calico-type designs—are charming when used with a dado. Simple wrought-iron chandeliers or wall brackets, brass

American eagle wall plaques, pewter mugs, and copper accessories are bright touches. Cottage-type curtains look well at the windows. In flooring patterns, sheet vinyl with the natural look of slate, brick, or cobblestone are appropriate, as are any of the pebbly textures or miniature chip designs.

**A cheery kitchen with bright colors and patterns makes for a pleasant working environment.**

A country-style kitchen.

**French Provincial.** Cabinets with the more ornate, scroll-like moldings, in either wood or antique painted finishes, are teamed with the country French, curved version of ladder-backed and other Provincial chairs. A plate rack or cupboard displaying delicate china or demitasse cups in the flower-sprigged Limoges manner is a charming addition. Wallpapers should be delicate in feeling, perhaps featuring small floral patterns. Cafe curtains on brass rods or organdy with ruffled tie-backs look nice at the windows. For the gay, hospitable look of the bistro, cover a round table with a checked cloth and accessorize with colorful vegetables or fruit in an elongated straw basket, tall wine bottles, and a cheese board.

**Mediterranean.** For the flavor of Spain, find some interesting chairs with carved and cut-out wood backs and a table with a solid, almost weighty feeling. Cabinets may be plain with a mellow, rich wood finish set off by paneled doors. A roughhewn beamed ceiling and white-painted rough-textured walls are especially good background touches. In flooring, the classic Spanish tile pattern, now available in a practical vinyl version, is perfect, either in natural terra cotta or a choice of other colors. Ceramic tile floors are also most appropriate. Curtains, tablecloths, and towels

might be striped in the bright colors of a Spanish or South American fiesta. For wall and shelf accessories, choose native pottery, decorative Spanish tiles, and a selection of copper and brass objects.

**Contemporary.** Studies in color and form are the substance of a contemporary kitchen. Cabinet finishes can be wood, with walnut or teak the favorites, or paint in imaginative hues—for example, yellow, curry, orange, used in succession to break the monotony of a row of identical doors. The table and chairs need not be one of those "kitchen-look" chrome dinette sets, as long as the table has a washable, stain- and scuff-proof top. Danish-inspired walnut or teak tables, protected by plastic-laminated tops, are excellent choices and can be teamed with matching wood chairs or any of the wonderful, washable molded plastic seating that comes in white, black, orange, and other colors. Garden or patio furniture brought indoors is a delight; wrought-iron sets with glass, or plastic-topped tables are especially practical and can be repainted in any color you choose. The floor can be the highlight of the room. In tile, checkerboard or harlequin patterns are effective either in elegant, understated black and white, or white with red, yellow, orange or any other color that

fits in best. Subtle, muted patterns are exciting when accented by bold feature strips—perhaps in the primary colors of red, blue, and yellow in a Mondrian pattern. Carpeting is also a wise selection for contemporary kitchens. Simple cafe or gathered curtains, window shades with a small amount of trim, or wood shutter panels with fabric insets are attractive window treatments. Modern lighting fixtures suspended like mobiles from the ceiling add interest. Japanese import stores, gift shops, and some department and summer furniture stores also stock interesting paper lanterns and a variety of rattan lamps and chandeliers.

## Color and Pattern

When planning the kitchen's color scheme, consider the sources of color. The walls, floor, ceiling, cabinets and countertop offer the largest areas of color. The appliances, sink, and dining furniture provide smaller, but still important, color sources, and the window curtains, chair cushions, canisters, towels, and even utensils contribute still more color. For the construction of a swatch board to evaluate your color scheme, see Chapter 14.

The kitchen is primarily a work area and it should be bright and colorful. Cool colors (blues and greens) are best for kitchens which get warm light from the south or west. Warm colors (reds, oranges, yellows) are more appropriate in kitchens which face north and east. Warm colors are best for manual tasks, and cool colors for relaxation and concentration. It doesn't follow, however, that because kitchens are work areas they shouldn't have blue or green color schemes. It does mean, though, that if a blue or green color scheme is used, the kitchen will need plenty of light—preferably a warm light. It's also true that too many bold, strong colors on the kitchen's largest surfaces will be unpleasant, over-stimulating and eye-straining. Bright, intense colors should be confined to smaller areas—an accent wall, window curtain, or accessories. As a general rule, the kitchen's largest surfaces are more acceptable in light or medium tones, while the smaller areas can be bolder and more intense.

As with all interior decorating, color and pattern work hand in hand in kitchen design. It's very important to remember the value of patterns in selecting an over-all color scheme. They can be a dramatic accent as well as a handy inspiration in choosing a good color scheme. Many a striking kitchen began with a swatch of cloth that combined several beautiful colors in an attractive pattern. The same colors can be simply picked up and extended throughout the kitchen with very happy results. When decorating, patterns can brighten, cover flaws, or unify a room chopped up with too many doors and windows.

Although today there is a trend of "freely" combining many patterns with great daring, some still-valid points which should be remembered when working with patterns in the kitchen are:

1. Be careful in using two stong patterns close together in large amounts. If the cabinet forms are already visually patterned, the addition of a patterned wall treatment could create visual confusion.

2. Be especially careful in using large-scale patterns. The size of the pattern should conform to the wall and other surface areas for which it will be used. On the other hand, the use of a supergraphic, which is a large pattern, can be very effective, if it is used carefully.

3. A window form or other opening which may interfere with the total harmony of the kitchen can be visually removed by tying it to its nearby surroundings with a pattern.

4. Large areas of strong pattern, such as the floor and countertops, can be very dominant, and are most effective when other patterns and textures remain supportive to it.

5. Repeat the dominant shapes that occur in the kitchen forms in the choice of fabric or wallcovering

A spacious kitchen with a truly distinctive touch.

patterns. If the dominant forms are geometric, a smaller-scaled geometric pattern with some subordinate curves would be a good choice. This procedure will aid in establishing harmony and unity.

## Other Kitchen Decorating Ideas

The usual furniture for the kitchen consists of cabinets, tables and chairs, and a high stool for chores that can be done while seated. By adding just one or two pieces of furniture, you can give your kitchen decorative distinction and perhaps extend the usefulness of the area as an all-around activity room.

For an accent piece that's both functional and decorative, try a quaint hutch that will hold some of your china, glass, silver, and linens, or a deacon's bench with cushion to match your curtains. An old desk, given a new finish to blend with the other woods or paint colors, can be the basis of a study, hobby, writing, or sewing center. If space is limited, use a wall-hung plate rack, a rocking chair in front of the window, or a butcher-block table as one of your work surfaces. Secondhand stores often yield treasures to those who have the imagination to introduce the unexpected into the workaday world of the kitchen—marble-topped chests of drawers to be sanded down and refinished or painted and decorated, swivel-type piano stools to replace the humdrum kitchen

**This economical use of space provides ample storage capacity and an uncluttered, easy-to-clean floor area.**

stool, or kindling boxes to hold magazines and double as benches.

Where there's no room at all for other than the conventional furniture, much can be done by substituting unusual accessories for those commercially available. Again, the secondhand shops are a spendid source, and so are the beaches or wooded areas surrounding your home.

Use the following list to get you thinking in the right direction, and try to come up with innovations of your own:

1. *Penny candy, apothecary, and other old jars.* Use several on a shelf over your sink to hold detergent, scouring powder, scouring pads, and other cleansers, thereby eliminating the eyesore of commercial packages without having to hide them in a cabinet. Glass jars are also attractive when filled with macaroni in different shapes.

2. *Framed prints.* Old botany prints, depicting fruits and vegetables and giving their Latin names, are appropriate for kitchens. So are reprints of famous still-life paintings that bring out the beauty of everyday kitchen objects—fruit, nuts, wine bottles, and loaves of bread.

3. *Nature's wonders.* A drive in the country can produce accessories to rival anything you'll find in a store. Almost every section of the country has something to offer that will last for at least a few weeks or months, if not longer—palm fronds, Spanish moss, pine cones, dried leaves, pussy willows, cattails, Indian corn, gourds, seashells, pebbles, and driftwood.

4. *Old farmhouse kitchen tools.* Wood or metal accessories add warmth and texture when used to decorate walls and shelves or when placed casually on tables and counters—salad bowls, butter presses, coffee grinders, spoons, spoon racks, kitchen scales, cookie molds, and trivets.

5. *China and glass collections.* For bringing brightness and cheer into a kitchen, few accessories can surpass a collection of colored glass placed in a sunny window. Artistically clustered demitasse cups, hand-decorated plates, or varied coffee mugs are also decorative.

When working with novel accessories, the temptation to be too whimsical may creep in occasionally, but this need not be a problem if you always bear in mind that a subtle hand is the key to good taste. If an

Accessories such as apothecary and other glass jars or novelties add spice to your kitchen decor.

old object is genuinely useful—like the apothecary jar that holds detergent—fine. If not, be content to admire it as is. Early telephones, stoves, coffee grinders, and spinning wheels take on a coy, commercial look that defeats their purpose when you try to make them useful by converting them into planters or transistor radios.

The decorative warmth you give a kitchen will, of course, in itself extend the room's usefulness by encouraging members of the family and their guests to gather there for games, card playing, or a snack. If kitchen chairs have padded seats and lighting is adequate, this might be the spot for messy hobbies not welcome elsewhere—like those requiring glue, paste, and oil paints or water color.

Providing facilities for other activities not related to the kitchen is fairly simple. A desk area is convenient for teen-agers to whom refrigerator raiding and studying are inseparable, or for a parent who needs space for menu planning, bill paying, or to do work brought home from the office. The desk need be no more than a wall-hung shelf, perhaps with a built-in file drawer or place to store writing equipment. A good reading lamp is essential.

A person who sews a great deal may wish to reserve a corner of the kitchen for himself or herself, particularly if there is a pull-down ironing board on the wall and one can enjoy the convenience of moving easily from sewing machine to ironing center. With either a portable typewriter that can be stored in the broom closet or a table-top machine that folds out of sight, the same surface can double as a writing or studying desk when sewing sessions are over.

The kitchen that is large enough may also be converted into a complete kitchen/family-room combination, where a parent can keep an eye on the children by day, and have companionship while doing the after-dinner tasks. This aspect is discussed in Chapter 9.

# FAMILY ROOMS AND dens

9

A casual life style, which began in the West and Southeast, has spread fairly rapidly across the country. In its wake are new, relaxed attitudes toward family living that have left a definite mark on our decorating attitudes. Rigid formality, which once greatly influenced our interior decorating styles, has given way to an easy-going informality. Nowhere is this more obvious than in the decorating of family rooms and dens (or studies).

Family rooms and dens, therefore, have a specific decorating mission. In the den, the sought-after mood is solitary relaxation and comfort; the family room is a cheerful, chatty locale for a gathering of family and friends. More than any other room, dens and family rooms offer the decorator the opportunity to project the personality of the family who is going to use these two areas. Yet remember, the watchwords in decorating these rooms are *leisure* and *comfort*—two elements that must be present in the interior design if it is to be a success.

## FAMILY ROOMS

A "family room" is what you make it—and you can make it anything you like. Consider the different connotations of just a few of the synonyms that might be substituted for "family room." A family room could be a "rumpus room," a "game room," a "recreation room," a "hobby room," or even a "work room." But, whatever its name, the family room is obviously the second living room, and an established fact in the hierarchy of the home. Other facts are also established: that it must be inviting to everyone,

family and friend alike; that it must cater to the leisure pursuits of each family member; that it must be bright and also eminently comfortable; that it must have some relationship, design-wise, with the rest of the house; and last, that it must be easily maintainable. Since the family room belongs to everyone, an at-

**A den is reserved for periods of private relaxation or study.**

tempt, in all fairness, should be made to please each member of the family without destroying the harmony of the end result. This is not as difficult as it sounds, particularly since you're dealing with a lighthearted, informal room that is supposed to reflect the excitement of several diverse personalities living as a unit.

One person's idea of solid comfort may be a huge leather chair, while another's may be a satin-upholstered French chaise longue. The combination is impossible, of course—yet one can sink just as comfortably into a large Colonial wing chair with provincial print slipcover, and the other can sit just as comfortably in a correlated smaller chair. Finding out each one's heart's desire, then making the necessary compromises, is all it takes to present a united front in the family room.

In style, the family room may be traditional or contemporary as long as the furnishings are sturdy, easy to care for, informal in feeling, and relatively "accident proof." The purpose of a family room is defeated when the occupants must obey a long list of "don'ts" that interferes with pleasurable relaxation. Try to incorporate as many washable mar-proof surfaces as possible—resilient flooring, laminated-plastic table tops, and easy-care fabrics. If your heart is set on an upholstery fabric that requires special cleaning, have

it treated with one of the stain-repellent finishes.

Gaining widespread popularity in recent years for indoor use in informal areas are the so-called "summer" or "outdoor" furniture designs. You can furnish an entire room with handsome rattan or wrought-iron or tubular metal sofas, chairs, tables, and occasional pieces that are suitably casual in feeling, easy to care for, and so light in weight that you can easily rearrange the room for parties, games, and other activities. Outdoor and casual designs also blend well when used as accent pieces with other types of furniture. A pair of woven rattan chairs, a wrought-iron table-and-chair set, or rattan tea cart in Oriental style are among the many selections which will fill in bare spots with furniture that is attractive, inexpensive, and functional.

In contemporary furniture, the relatively maintenance-free studio couches—slabs of foam sheathed in washable, zip-off fabrics—are favorites for family rooms because they are comfortable for sitting or sleeping as well as practical and inexpensive. You can even make your own sofa with a flush door, a set of legs, foam mattress, bolsters, and fabric for slipcovers. The budget-minded can then round out the room with unpainted cabinets and ready-made shelving for storage, colorful molded-plastic or summer-furni-

A family room should try to accommodate the tastes and interests of every member of the unit.

**The fireplace and small bar provide an intimate touch.**

ture-department chairs, and a few tables with laminated-plastic tops.

The styles of other centuries and of a variety of foreign countries are also possibilities for combining warmth and good cheer with practicality. Early American and Colonial furniture are pleasantly informal and offer an especially good solution for the decorating problems of the combined kitchen/family room. Country French furniture, depending on the fabrics and background used with it, can evoke a variety of decorating moods ranging from rustic to sophisticated. By choosing a Mediterranean theme, lovers of tradition find they can establish the necessary air of informality, yet enjoy the richness of carved woods and solid, substantial furniture.

Comfortable seating for everyone is the primary requisite of a family room that will be used for hours of watching television, reading, talking, and other quiet pursuits, Since a sofa is apt to be preempted by someone for a nap, groupings that include twin studio couches or sectionals, love seats, and additional chairs should be considered. If watching television is a favorite pastime, the seating arrangement will naturally be geared to the set. Reading and sewing should also be provided for by including lamps that give over-the-shoulder light at both ends of the sofa and next to easy chairs.

When it's impossible to find the one arrangement satisfactory for all "sitting down" activities, try to buy furniture that is easy to move, or use casters on heavier pieces. If the room includes a dining area, for auxiliary seating, rely on side chairs or inexpensive and light-weight rattan, canvas, or other casual furniture.

The entertainment center, a vital part of the family room, can be as simple and inexpensive as a combination television-stereo unit and a place to keep records or tapes. On the other hand, it may be lavish, expensive, and all-encompassing—color television, stereo with maze of component parts, tape recorder, bar cabinet, and every up-to-the-minute advancement—in the quest for getting more out of leisure time.

Housing entertainment facilities in a series of cabinets, then continuing up the wall with shelves and other storage, is a favorite device for making economical use of available space in the family room that must fulfill a long list of requirements. Where budget is to be considered, unpainted cabinets can be purchased to hold phonograph, television set, and related equipment. When painted or antiqued and perhaps trimmed with decorative moldings and fancier hardware, these cabinets undergo a remarkable transformation into good-looking finished furniture.

In more and more homes, the family room is becoming the preferred location for the main meal of the day. Even if this is not the case in your home, you'll probably want a dining table and chairs for card games, late suppers, brunches, buffet dinners, or serving the children while you entertain adults in the dining room. If the family room is far from the kitchen, consider installing a pullman-type kitchen, such as those often used in efficiency apartments—sink, small refrigerator, with a two-burner cooking top, and cabinet space.

The shape and design of the table is important for reasons both practical and aesthetic. Remember that this is a multipurpose room in which compromises must be made if all areas are to function smoothly. If the placement of your main seating group, entertainment center, and other facilities leaves inadequate floor space for a complete dining area, it is best to rely on other alternatives—buffet suppers set up on an extension table, and meals served from snack trays or folding card tables. But before deciding on the shape of a dining table, visualize the total look of the room. If most of the furniture is rectangular, a round or oval table may be the most pleasing. Think of alternate uses, too; a round table creates a friendly atmosphere for card games.

Some pieces of furniture for rumpus or family room use are rather specialized. For instance, recreational

A spacious bar is a good investment if you entertain large numbers of guests at a time.

equipment like a billiard table, or if the room is smaller, a bumper-pool table is almost a "must" for a rumpus or family room. Other recreational room furniture may include a dry bar (a good substitute for a wet bar and it requires less space), and an old player piano or organ. Neither of the latter has to work to be effective; just stick one in the corner, load it down with old sheet music, and it will radiate charm.

The over-all goal in designing family-room interiors is to involve the whole family. Put in something for everyone: a chessboard, a stereo system, television, family games—anything that conveys the fact that this is where the family congregates and enjoys one another.

Color—an especially important element in the family room—can supply much of the warmth and vitality that is an integral part of the over-all decorating scheme. Use color to express the mood that best sums up your collective personality—vibrant colors for an outgoing group who like a busy, noisy family room; cheerful but subtle hues for those who prefer to relax in quiet surroundings; bold accents on a subdued background for the well-rounded ones who strike a happy medium. Be bright, gay, and lighthearted in your approach to color—but, if you plan to spend a lot of time within those four walls, avoid too much brilliance in large doses. The impact of hot pinks, oranges, and other vibrant hues can be charm-

ing if limited to small area rugs and other accessories. Respect, too, the pet likes and dislikes of other family members, and strive to please everyone. But, whether you prefer the light and airy look of contemporary design or the more substantial charm of period decor, it is the many smaller decisions you'll be called upon to make—like choosing flooring, wallcoverings, fabrics, area rugs, and other accessories—that will determine the success of your family room as a place to get the most enjoyment out of leisure time.

The flooring alone can contribute much to the over-all look a family room should have—a study in gracious living where beauty, comfort, and practicality share equal honors. An expanse of seamless vinyl is especially suitable to give a look of unity to a room that is usually divided into two, three, or even more separate areas of activity—seating, dining, home entertainment, study, and children's play areas. In larger family rooms, the main area of activity can be separated by using the same flooring pattern in another color, or by outlining with an inlaid strip of solid-colored vinyl.

Colorful accent rugs are another excellent means of bringing harmony to a large multipurpose room. You might, for example, select a rectangular area rug to underscore a conversation grouping, then outline a round dining table and chairs with a harmonizing circular or hexagonal rug. In small sizes, these rugs are easy to clean. Some may be tossed into the washing machine.

The walls and ceiling, too, play a major role in bringing beauty, color, and individuality into a room. Wood paneling is always appropriate for the warmth and richness it lends to an informal atmosphere. Also appropriate are painted walls with a rough-textured look, or patterned wallpapers or fabric coverings. To set off one wall, striped mattress ticking, felt, or burlap are attractive, inexpensive coverings, and the color choice is wide for the last two. An acoustical ceiling is helpful, particularly if the room will be used for entertaining or late television viewing by some members of the family while others are sleeping or studying elsewhere.

Window coverings should be simple, yet distinctive. Curtains made from cotton, sailcloth, denim, and other washable fabrics take on an expensive custom look when trimmed to pick up the room's colors and patterns.

Accessorizing the family room provides a real opportunity for self-expression. This is the place for displaying treasured family photographs, sports trophies, and other personal mementos that might seem out of place in more formal living areas. Let good taste be your guide, however, and refrain from being whimsical or too obvious. The family whose hobby is boating, for example, might enhance the decor of the room with a collection of model sailing ships, a framed photograph of their own boat, and perhaps a display of trophies won in sailing races. Simulating the interior of a cabin, however, by hanging up life preservers and fish nets, will soon bore everyone.

## DENS

Designing a den is a special challenge all its own. The den, quite often used as an additional bedroom, is usually a retreat. Make it private, reclusive almost— a cozy and comfortable escape. Translating comfort into color means using warm-toned hues, shutters, paneling, perhaps a desk, and floor-to-ceiling bookcases.

Comfort can be achieved using a wide range of furnishings. Select from massive, traditional, French Provincial, or sleek chrome-and-glass furniture. All can be used successfully, giving the den a particular ambiance.

Accessorizing contributes heavily to this ambiance, for it sets a definite mood. Accessories tell you something about the person whose room it is. For instance,

**Accessories which reflect a family hobby such as boating should please everyone.**

enlarged, mounted black-and-white photographs, a camera tripod, and a scattering of prints obviously indicate that the user of the room is a camera buff. If it's going to be used as a sewing room, the sewing machine, an old wire mannequin, bolts of material, or patterns can be used. But, the most important factor of any den is an atmosphere of serenity and privacy. This atmosphere is created by more than actual noise-buffering accouterments—a heavy door, acoustical ceiling, thick, sound-absorbing carpet and draperies.

Quiet, as a state of mind, is also evoked by a relaxing scheme of decoration. The decorative ambiance one finds restful is the most important ingredient in a retreat. Evolve a scheme which feels warm, restful, human, and lived-in, whether it be with wood paneling and leather upholstery, a neutral color scheme or, perhaps, a floral motif. To be relaxing, a den must also be functional, with specialized storage to prevent clutter, good lighting, and the proper furniture—a desk, chair, and bookcase are essentials, often combined with sofas and chairs. Where space is at a premium, a den can be tucked into a corner.

# bedrooms
# 10

A bedroom is more than a bed and a place for sleeping. In most homes, bedrooms are regarded as private domains, faithful reflections of their occupants. While the rooms we have been considering—the living room, dining area, and kitchen—share a common semi-public character, a bedroom is private property, it only makes such concessions to the general scheme of things as its owner cares to make. Possibly it sounds old-fashioned, but with privacy fast becoming a luxury, the distinction between the bedroom and the openly hospitable and the more intimate parts of a home should be fostered as much as possible.

As living quarters grow smaller in today's homes, each bedroom deserves more attention as a possible source of bonus living space. For instance, bedrooms that can do double duty are the teen bedroom/guest room, den-library/guest room, child's room/playroom, and the multi-function master suite. Thus, whether you're assigning uses to bedrooms in a mansion or a one-bedroom apartment, you'll find it helpful to key your interior design and furnishing plans to type of use—active or quiet; mood—practical or esoteric; and budget—nominal or luxurious or anything in between.

## MASTER BEDROOM

The master bedroom is what you see the first thing in the morning and last at night, and for those two reasons alone it should be the room that best expresses your most intimate and personal preferences. Luxurious or sparse, romantic, dramatic or cozy—all are wonderfully appropriate bedroom styles so long as the mood is peaceful and comfortable.

The whole function of the master bedroom has been going through subtle changes. No longer is it just a place where people go at the end of a long day. Rather, especially when children are in the home, parents are using it as a retreat. More and more waking hours are spent there and it has become sort of a private rest and relaxation area. The right furnishings will turn the bedroom into a place to write letters and pay bills; read; do needlepoint; listen to your favorite music; build a healthier body through exercise; or simply to retreat into your own aloneness.

The evolution of the use of the master bedroom is

**Multi-function child's bedroom with ample provision for storage. Private dining, too.**

**The master bedroom is your private refuge and can be an expression of your most personal tastes.**

rather easy to follow. During the '30s and '40s, there was not as much time to relax as there is now in today's world of convenience foods and time-saving appliances. The bedroom was little more than a place to rest one's weary head and sleep. Entertainment was usually centered around the living room, listening to the radio.

The '50s and early '60s marked the beginning of the television era. As the popularity of television grew, relatively inexpensive sets became available, and today it is not uncommon for a family to have two, three, or even more television sets in the home. Family entertainment is no longer centered in one area of the home. As the use of television in the bedroom has grown, the result has been that people are spending more time there. Today, in many master bedrooms, you find more than just a bed and chest of drawers. Even the size of bedrooms has changed. Bedrooms are being designed bigger and bigger. It is now an area of the home where adults can sit and relax and sip their coffee or brandy and enjoy relaxed conversation.

There are many ways of decorating a bedroom, but the main objective should be to create a feeling of intimacy or, in other words, an area of solitude and comfort essentially off-limits to other members of the family—sort of a private combination bedroom/living room.

Since the master bedroom is shared, decorating it presents a slight challenge. The mood should be one that is warm, soothing, and somewhat seductive, yet one which is neither too masculine nor too feminine, making either a man or a woman feel out of place. A couple can generally decide on colors they both like, and find stripes or textures in this color range which will be acceptable to both of them. Master bedrooms should strive for a tailored look, with valances over the windows, ample draperies, and simple but comfortable furniture. Restraint with comfort might be the watchwords.

In a large bedroom, there may even be "his" and "her" sections, furnished more to each individual's taste, although the best solution is to have separate dressing rooms. Here the background and the appointments can differ from the bedroom proper to the degree that they are isolated from it. (Bathrooms adjacent to the bedroom are dealt with in the next chapter.)

When designing master-bedroom interiors, be sure to consider the bed, the obvious focal point of the room. Wherever possible, employ a queen-size; and if there is enough room, use a king-size. While twin

and double sizes are still being used—especially by older people—today's bigger, taller people require bigger, more spacious bedding. More than a third of all popular-priced bedding is now in super-size ranges, and half the sales of better bedding are in the same category. It is predicted that all bedding will eventually be in this larger range.

Super-size bedding is longer and wider; it must be 75 to 80 inches long to qualify as super-size. Queen-size bedding, which replaces the old full or double size, is 60 inches wide; and king size is 76 inches wide. "California" kings are 72 inches wide, 84 inches long. Anyone who is at least 5 ½ feet tall needs a queen-size (60 inches wide, 80 to 84 inches long) or a king-size (76 to 78 inches wide, 80 to 84 inches long) bed. This provides the 5 inches at both head and foot that let one stretch out comfortably on the bed. If the bed's occupant is closer to six feet tall, the extra-long (84 inches) bed is advisable. Another way to view it is that the bed should be 6 to 10 inches longer than the height of the tallest occupant who regularly sleeps in it.

Some designers prefer to emphasize the bed to add a dramatic touch, and will even go so far as to elevate the bed by placing it on a 6-inch platform. Others would rather underplay the bed and nighttime role of the room. The latter can be accomplished both by coverings—substituting upholstery-like fabrics for flossy bedspreads—and by placement. Begin the conversion of your old-fashioned bedroom by devising a bed arrangement that will leave room for furniture more usually found in living room or study. Discard your matching night stands for other pieces that will serve the same purpose, yet fit more harmoniously into the new decor. A bedside reading lamp, for instance, can be placed equally well upon a small round table sheathed in a floor-length felt skirt, on a handsome commode, or even on a small desk.

It's not essential that twin beds be lined up, side by side, gobbling space by projecting into the room; nor is it necessary that a double, queen- or king-size bed dominate the entire floor area. A technique employed for centuries by the French is to recess the bed, regardless of size, into a fitted niche in the wall. The effect can be grand, with elegant hangings topped by a valance stretching across the entire alcove; or starkly modern, with a tailored cover and piles of pillows turning the bed into an inviting form

of seating. Since few American homes boast the requisite niche, you can provide your own by building walk-in closets on each side. If your room is sufficiently large, one closet might be replaced by an extra bath. If your room is small, a corner of the wall can serve as one side of the niche.

The furniture to be added as companions to the beds will depend, of course, upon personal tastes and individual activities. The avid reader may desire an easy chair and footstool, and voluminous shelves for books and periodicals. The collector may line the walls with glass-fronted display cabinets—treasures thus tucked away offer no temptations to the tiny tots in the house.

A desk may be a desirable addition for handling household accounts, records for the PTA, secretarial work, homework from the job, or for laying out, undisturbed, a stamp collection. A laminated-plastic-topped counter may be the realization of a dream to the parent whose hobby is wood carving, clay sculpture, or jewelry making. So, too, would be an easel and a cabinet for art supplies for a painter. Such a private art center, unlike makeshifts in kitchen or dining room, would afford the amateur artist the privilege, when interrupted by other duties, of leaving the unfinished work and its resultant clutter undisturbed until he or she returns. Many master bedrooms now combine bath and sauna-exercise area, thus permitting body-building activities to be carried on in private.

## CHILDREN'S BEDROOMS

Young children, especially, need a place where they can play without having to be careful of an expensive lamp or wary of getting into things that don't belong to them. For older children, a room designed to be used by day satisfies a normal craving for occasional privacy and a place in which to enjoy one's own possessions. The teen-ager will benefit from having a room where he can bring his friends for bull sessions, practice the guitar, cram for exams, or spend the inevitable hours of music appreciation the rest of the family can't bear.

Particularly for families living in apartments or in small homes with limited space, it is important for various members to have a place for pursuing their own private interests. Homemakers who lack the space for following the usual modern formulas for family harmony—the separate playroom or the recreation room—can find answers to their own particular problems by providing multi-function sleeping rooms, not only for youngsters, but, as already men-

**(Top) A single bedroom with a combination bureau and dressing table. (Bottom) Master bedroom with breakfast nook.**

tioned, for adults as well.

With some careful planning on your part, many of the same basic furnishings you buy for your tot can still be in use when he becomes a teen-ager. Buying for children's rooms should be done in the same way as for the rest of the house—spend as much as you can on items that give years of service, and as little as you can on those items suitable for only one stage of a child's growth. Here are some suggestions on where to find the right furniture.

**Juvenile furniture stores or departments.** Some manufacturers offer nursery furniture that really grows with the child, such as modular units that you can add to as the child requires more storage space and acquires a roommate; wall-hung furniture that can be moved higher as the child grows taller; and cabinets with adjustable fittings all ready for the trading of baby clothes for sports equipment and games. On the other hand, avoid those scaled-down units reminiscent of dollhouse furniture. Even if you repaint them and change the hardware, they will still retain the telltale "baby" look a school-age youngster will deplore. Well-designed juvenile furniture is compact but not miniature, and free of "gingerbread" details and curves that cheapen its appearance.

**Adult furniture.** In this era when smaller room sizes have necessitated compact furniture design, there are dozens of choices in regular furniture departments that adapt remarkably well to juvenile requirements. Clean-lined contemporary design, the simple charm of Early American, the warmth of French and Italian Provincial adaptations—all these are suited to juvenile decorating themes. Many chests and tables have mar-proof plastic tops or other special finishes.

**Unpainted furniture.** A bonanza to the budget-minded is the unpainted furniture department—and nothing could be more suitable for children of all ages. You can start with one or two pieces, then add on as the need develops. These units—dressers, chests, bookcases, desks—can be lined up side by side, or stacked to save floor space. With a fresh coat of paint, you can change a color scheme and make older pieces look the same as new additions. Although drawer knobs and cabinet hardware come with your purchases, buying your own decorative hardware gives a custom touch and a look of quality.

**Summer and casual furniture.** For reasons of economy, ease of care, and adaptability to young decorating themes, the summer-furniture department is another excellent source. Much indoor-outdoor furniture is light in weight, bright in color and interesting in design. You wouldn't want a room full of it, of course, but one or two accent pieces will bring a spark of excitement indoors. An outdoor dining table with laminated-plastic or metal top makes a sturdy play table. In chairs there are many choices—canvas, rattan, and molded plastic. Also interesting are wicker baskets for use as toy chests, and rattan headboards you can paint any color.

**Secondhand furniture.** While "junk shop" furniture may be used all through the house, it's particularly easy to fit these treasures into juvenile rooms, where the charm and whimsy of your decorating scheme minimizes any defects. When buying secondhand pieces, be sure there's a minimum of expense and labor involved in restoring them. Unless your child's room is larger than average, steer clear of those big, cumbersome chests and bureaus that are out of scale with today's interior dimensions.

**Built-in furniture.** Shelves, bookcases, wall-hung desks, cabinets, and other built-ins are almost a necessity if much of your child's room is to be given over to an uncluttered, appealing, play and study area. Often you can find what you want at a large department store. Other alternatives are to call in a carpenter and have everything made to order, or tackle some simple carpentry yourself. Having enough

**Drawers for storage under the bed are an excellent space saver.**

(Left and below) Ideas that give children's rooms a little extra.

131

## Beds

The choice of beds is important if a room is to be really useful during the daytime. When a child has his or her own room, it's a simple matter to purchase a twin bed and disguise it as a studio couch with a pretty throw and lots of toss pillows. Where two or more children must share a room, consider one of these possibilities:

**Bunk beds.** These beds are usually stacked in double-decker fashion, giving sleeping accommodations for two in the space of one. They also lend themselves to such decorating whimsy as a Western bunkhouse, a cabin in the woods, or the interior of a choo-choo train complete with pullman car. If you're leery of having one child in the upper bunk or think bed-making will be a nuisance, you can take stacked bunk beds apart and place them end-to-end along one wall and still have room to spare.

**Storage-bin bed combinations.** Instead of the usual bed frames, have a local carpenter build twin storage units with drawers, in the dimensions of your mattresses, which can then be placed on top. This gives a trim, studio look to a room and enables you to get away with fewer pieces of furniture, since you'll have plenty of extra drawer space under both beds.

**Trundle beds.** One bed rolls out from under the other in this old-fashioned idea revived to suit modern living. Trundle beds are good looking and come in traditional styles that are charming for young people.

Practical flooring is an absolute must for youngsters' rooms. Tiny tots need a place where they can spill milk, scatter cookie crumbs, and ride wheel toys without the floor being any the worse for wear. Older youngsters are apt to treat the floor as a gymnasium and wrestling arena, while teen-agers are merciless in their frenetic interpretations of the latest dance steps.

drawers and shelves in the right sizes to accommodate outsize picture books and bulky games, will make it easier for your child to straighten his own room at the end of a day's play. But, be sure to include the closet in your plans for saving floor space. With built-in shoe racks, shelves, and double tiers of clothes poles for hanging twice as many small garments, even a modestly proportioned closet can yield more storage space than you may have thought possible.

Adaptable boy's bedroom.

While wall-to-wall carpeting is usually considered ideal for the master-bedroom, carefree resilient vinyl flooring is best for children's bedrooms.

While it is possible with versatile resilient flooring to create special effects in floor patterns—inlaid animal cutouts, nursery-rhyme figures, or a background for checkers and hopscotch—remember that long-wearing vinyl flooring materials will usually outlive the stages of your children's growth. When budget is a consideration, it's best to be more conventional, just adding a juvenile scatter rug or two as an accent for your decorating theme, perhaps in a gay pattern depicting animals, circus performers, or nursery-rhyme characters. Later, these old rugs can be replaced to suit the surroundings of an older child, such as fake animal skins or plush, synthetic-fur accent rugs.

In choosing a color for a young child's floor, there is no need to limit yourself to pink, blue, or other pastels. From the time they are able to see, children are attracted and delighted by the more vibrant colors in the chromatic scale. With either a neutral floor or a pattern that contains multicolored flecks, you have an excellent basis for changing the color scheme as your child goes through successive stages of growth.

There are so many themes to delight youngsters that lack of an idea need never be a problem. Just remember that in decorating, one idea is better than two or three; so once you decide on a theme, stay with it. To start with a circus motif and later introduce a few nautical accessories is no less a mistake than mixing Louis XIV with Early American.

Another important point to consider is the longevity of your theme in relation to its cost. Mother Goose stories and other nursery ideas are fun to carry out, but since they will be short lived, don't invest too much of your time or money on them—unless you plan them in such a way that the original idea can be adapted to something else as the child grows older.

For example, what started as a six-year-old's bunk-

**Ruffles and flowers give a distinctly feminine touch for a girl's bedroom.**

house can make a transition into a camplike atmosphere. In the teen years, the same background with new accessories will suit either a sports-minded girl or boy who loves horseback riding, or one who enjoys studies and nature hobbies in a rustic cabin setting. It is only by thinking of the future that you can be sure any theme will be sufficiently flexible to mature with your child. Several examples of children's bedroom themes are shown in this chapter.

## Guest Rooms

Just as children's bedrooms must be made to yield daytime dividends, so should a guest room be useful to the family on a year-round basis. After all, few of us entertain overnight guests more than a fraction of the time, and it's hardly practical in this age of cramped quarters to give over a room completely to a part-time function.

A dual-purpose room works best when you plan from the very beginning to accommodate both functions, rather than attempt to impose a second usage upon a room that is already established. In choosing which space in your home would best lend itself to this sort of versatility, it is important to consider both the personalities and the individual needs of the various members of your family.

A guest bedroom can double as a sewing room, hobby corner, music center, recreation room, den, library, or as a general-purpose retreat to be used by any member of the family when he or she requires privacy. Before deciding upon its second function, however, try to anticipate the effects upon family living patterns during periods when the room is given over to its role as a guest room. If your study is actually a home office essential to daily business, it is not feasible to displace this activity for the sake of guests. Nor, when your children are small, is it logical to try to banish them at intervals from a playroom which they consider their own exclusive domain.

The choosing of furnishings for double-duty rooms has been greatly facilitated in recent years by furniture designers who recognize the space limitations of modern quarters. Acquaint yourself with these aids before beginning your planning. Dual-function sleeping designs include, of course, the time-honored fold-out studio couch and the single beds that nest, trundle-style, one beneath the other; there are also beautifully-styled convertible sofas, love seats, chairs, and even hassocks. Your choice will depend not only upon available space, but also upon the

**This room could serve equally well as a twin bedroom or guest room.**

number of guests you expect to entertain simultaneously. Storage pieces, too, offer twin usages. A desk featuring a lift-up lid mirrored on the underside may serve handsomely as a vanity table for your guests; an end table may be, in reality, a file cabinet.

Design advances in executive office furniture now make this long-stagnant field an exciting source of double-duty furnishings. For those who may be using the guest room for free-lance work at home, for instance, there are file cabinets resembling sleek-lined chests of drawers. Such pieces are a boon to hostesses who consider the daily clutter necessary to their work an insult to their guests when it is left lying around in disorder during overnight visits.

Putting your guests at ease involves more than a gracious greeting upon their arrival. The well-appointed guest room offers a more meaningful welcome, and strikes a happy medium between the overly elegant and the carelessly sloppy. Priceless antiques and precious porcelains tend to keep a guest uncomfortable and continually on guard; on the other hand, wear-weary cast-offs from the rest of the house place a low evaluation upon your guest's status. There, let common sense be your guide. If your guest room is also a hobby room, for instance, place your rare collections in cabinets or frame them for protection. Consider the advantages of mar-proof furniture, stain-repellent fabrics, plate-glass covers for vulnerable surafces; all aid in minimizing accidents. Hostess ire or guest remorse can spoil a visit.

Like any dual-purpose room, a guest room should have an especially good floor plan. A common error in arranging studio-type rooms is that of failing to allow opening-out room for convertible furniture. This is particularly true of sleeping units. Not only must there be space for the bed to open, but also an adequate margin must be allowed around the perimeter for comfortable access.

Often the function of furnishings can be multiplied by their placement. A combination vanity-desk can also serve as a lamp table by the simple expedient of positioning it at the end of the bed, at right angles to the wall. A cedar chest, sandwiched beneath a window between two chests of drawers, requires only a pad and cushions to double as a window seat, obviating more space-consuming seating.

Twin beds are handy in guest rooms, especially where increased sleeping space is required. For instance, twin beds, particularly those with low head- and footboards of equal height, can also be given a French look by simply placing the long side of the bed against the wall, putting tailored bolsters across each end of the bed, and piling cushions at the back.

Hollywood-style twin beds, with no foot- or headboards are even easier to arrange, offering great flexibility in their placement. Try a right-angle grouping, with the end of each bed abutting a large, square corner table. Or place the beds like sofas against opposite walls, each with a flanking chair or lamp table in the manner of conventional sofa arrangements.

Built-ins are often an admirable solution to small bedroom space problems. If custom-built units do not fit into your budget, you can often create the effect of built-ins by combining ready-made storage pieces with attractive shelving. Use matching or harmonizing colors to visually coordinate the various pieces, and further tie them together with a counter—either wood or laminated plastic—stretching over all base pieces. Wall-hung furniture such as desks, bars, or cabinets, are also useful for adding a more spacious look to cramped quarters.

# bathrooms

# 11

Whenever you are decorating the bathroom of your home, the one word to keep in mind is "glamour." There is nothing as drab as a plain white-walled bathroom with a sink, tub, and commode. There are no rules that say your bathroom has to look like a service-station restroom. Therefore, why not make it cheerful and bright?

Use colors, fabrics, patterns, and accessories generously. For example, in the master bathroom, put space to work by using countertops and shelves around the tub and sink. These are excellent for displaying a wide range of items such as bowls of colored and scented soaps, unique-shaped bottles and, of course, live plants. Don't forget the walls, either. Framed pictures or posters add to the decorative theme here, too. If the bathroom has a window, have the shade made from the wallcovering used on the walls.

The powder room is another very good place to try decorating ideas you have always wanted to use before, but never dared to try. Since no one stays in the room very long, you can be much more dashing here than in any other room in the house. This room is usually small, so you can follow either of two courses in selecting your wallcovering; you can use a see-through type of pattern, such as a caning or trellis design, or you can have fun, using a bold, zippy pattern that takes over the whole room. Mirrored walls are a great visual spacemaker, and overcome the claustrophobic effect of a small room. In fact, the bathroom is the one room in a home where mirroring can be used almost without limit. Mirroring on three sides of a

bathtub is permissible if the budget permits. Also keep in mind that plenty of plants and mirrors give a bathroom a sort of private-garden quality, where the day's tribulations can be locked out while resting in a comfortable bath.

When decorating a bathroom, you should determine the mood or feeling you are ultimately going to create. Do you prefer a setting that is traditional or

**There are many ways to add glamour to your bathroom. Ceiling, floor, walls, shower curtain, towels and accessories offer many possibilities.**

An interesting period chair, Tiffany-style lamp and decorative rattan screen add style to this bathroom.

contemporary, formal or informal, French Provincial or Mediterranean? It doesn't really matter what you choose. What is important is that you be consistent. Nothing could be prettier, for instance, than a warm French Provincial bathroom in a French Provincial home; on the other hand, an extremely contemporary bathroom in an authentically styled and decorated Colonial house is something of a jolt.

Color is your best ally in a bathroom. While the wallcovering pattern doesn't have to match other patterns in the bathroom such as towels, the colors should definitely match. Colors of countertop items also should match the wallcovering, no matter what size or shape the items may be. Remember, that since a bathroom requires fairly strong lights, light colors are frequently superfluous. Find out how restful dark walls can be, and how flattering both to you and to the room itself.

When redecorating an old bathroom, existing colored tile can be a problem. Often vile to look at, costly to remove, and unsatisfactory when painted over, the best way to fight color is with more color. Here are a few suggestions. That frightful favorite of the '20s and '30s—jade green and black—can be modified with walls in softer or deeper greens. For example, one could use shiki or moire silk vinyl, tone-on-tone damask, green flock on a green ground, or an over-all pattern of green leaves printed on white vinyl. A black

floor would help. Then there is peach tile with a brown trim, another "peachy" jazz-age tile combination. With this one you had better go in the direction of gold, more brown, and the warm neutrals, bearing in mind such textures as tortoise shell, marbleizing, and tweeds. Finally, you can probably take orchid tiles in stride if you accept their saccharine color and add violets and black-and-white butterflies, or multicolored candy stripes, including purple, which will make the orchid tiles look pink.

By comparison, really old bathrooms *sans* tile are easy to cope with. Their wood can be plastered over or covered with gypsum board and then given any wallcovering treatment desired. Also, if you have a tub with ball-and-claw feet on it, the exposed iron sides are an invitation to a bright floral pattern. We know there are various opinions about how "amusing" an interior ought to be, but surely if one puts up with inconvenience, one deserves a little innocent amusement. Wallpaper is wonderful for poking fun, occasionally, at the more pretentious forms of decorating. The sole requirement—when you're covering that hamper or garbage pail with rosebuds—is neatness. The light touch lacks wit if the hand is clumsy.

If you're remodeling a bathroom completely, there is a great deal that can be done. For instance, compartmented baths are popular with families with growing children. The addition of one or two fixtures

makes the bathroom look smaller. Solid-colored tile has the same effect in the bathroom that wall-to-wall carpeting has in any other room of the house; it gives an unbroken expanse of color, which makes the bathroom appear larger. As a matter of fact, wall-to-wall carpeting is no longer a rarity for the bathroom itself. It is practical as well as rich-looking, and it can make a fairly minimal bath seem almost luxurious, as well as larger.

Two more tips on space: To make a small wash basin look bigger, and certainly more glamorous, surround it with a countertop. And remember that a luminous ceiling stretches space overhead just as a solid-colored floor does underfoot.

Today's bathroom demands good lighting—both general and task—not only for vision and safety, but also for decorative enhancement. True, in a small powder room, with just a commode and vanity, a well-lighted mirror will usually provide sufficient brightness for the entire room. But for the larger bath, general lighting must be included as well.

The general bathroom light, for vision and safety, should include one ceiling fixture, recessed or surface-mounted, containing one 100-watt, or two 60-watt bulbs. For make-up and for shaving, there should be bathroom-mirror lighting as well. The mirror

and the multiple use of others add convenience and flexibility. In remodeling a bathroom a compartmented bath often makes the best use of space, particularly if a large area is being converted into a bathroom. That is, compartmenting can go a long way toward easing the bathroom bottleneck. The basic idea is to separate functional areas so that one person doesn't enter the bathroom, close the door, and tie up everything.

A compartmented bathroom allows others to use the facilities not being used by the person who got there first. It is the best way yet to get the children off to school in the morning. Minimal compartmenting, almost a must in the one-bathroom house, amounts to separating toilet from bath and vanity area. There are all kinds of practical and attractive dividers, from opaque glass to louvered doors, that can be used for this purpose; and the doors really must be sliding or folding to make the most of a little space. Enclosing the tub area with a sliding glass door, for example, can double the function of a bathroom without taking up an inch of extra space. In fact, you can get the effect of two full baths in a relatively limited area by using two toilets, two lavatories, and one tub, the tub being the most expensive item.

One way to counteract the feeling of smallness in such bathrooms, as stated earlier, is to use mirrors, mirrors, and more mirrors. Another small-bathroom trick involves tiling. A patterned ceramic tile floor

**(Top) Two well-decorated powder rooms. (Bottom) Bathrooms can be given period style.**

should be flanked by linear fixtures —either two 40-watt incandescent bulbs or one 20-watt fluorescent tube on each side. An increasingly popular innovation in bathroom lighting is theatrical lighting—framing the mirror on two, three, or four sides by a row of 25-watt incandescent bulbs.

Some new designs in theatrical lighting include:

1. Thin strips of polished chrome or brass, studded with frosted bulbs.

2. Chunky cubes of glass, centered with tiny bulbs.

3. Sculptural glass forms, containing the light source. Many models have switches which adjust from indoor to outdoor incandescent lighting, or evening fluorescent lighting—for the proper application of make-up for various settings. The chief advantage of such lighting is that it provides well-distributed illumination on all sides of the face and hands, so that a woman can apply make-up in a clear over-all light, and a man shave without the problem of misleading shadows.

Incandescent lighting, as mentioned in Chapter 2, is most like natural light, and the best for grooming needs. If fluorescent lighting is selected, deluxe warm white and natural white have the most rosy shades, and so are the most flattering to skin tones.

There can be so many variations in bathroom categories and styles that it's impossible to cover all the possibilities in this book. When you consider that bathroom design can be luxurious or economical, elegant or utilitarian, masculine or feminine, colorful or subtle, conservative or modern, it becomes apparent that only your budget, personal preferences, the number of individuals in your family, and the use planned for the bath facility affect the final interior design of your bathroom. Actually, the word "bathroom" may be a misnomer; you may really be planning a cosmetic center, a "mud" room, an exercise and health center, a combination bath and utility room, a master bathroom, a facility for several youngsters, a guest powder room; the list is endless. No bathroom can be all these things, so the first thing to do when you plan the design is to consider its prime purpose and the people who will be using it. Next, consider how to decorate it and put more life into this room for them. For instance, a powder room that will be used mostly by adult guests can be as lavish and luxurious as you care to make it. A bathroom to be used by two youngsters should be more practical. And when decorating the master bathroom, the quest for luxury and glamour should be paramount. Everyone treasures the privacy of the bathroom, and this privacy should be a pleasant experience.

An example of a truly luxurious bathroom complete with sunken tub.

# OTHER
# rooms

12

There are many "other rooms" in many homes. There are entrance, basement, attic, and garage rooms. These areas, in some cases, can be put to many of the purposes already mentioned; but frequently, they require special decorating techniques.

Remember that just because a space is not large enough to be called a room, there is no reason to forget it completely. Properly decorated, these small areas can become very important parts of any home. For example, a fairly large space under a staircase can frequently act as a "waiting room." Or a good-sized stair landing, furnished with bookshelves and a chair, may well serve as just the spot for reading. In fact, large halls are often made to do double duty. For example, a large foyer may be the home for a small piano and its accompanying bench. An apartment foyer can have a narrow table with banquettes along one side used for dining. A wide center hall in a spacious home can sometimes be transformed into a study or sewing center, or be just the place in which to create more closet space. Of course, one of the frequent charms of older homes is the number of small rooms tucked away in odd locales, that were used as servant's quarters. With a little thought and imagination these rooms can be transformed into hideaways like a den or some other "special" room.

## ENTRANCE AND HALLWAYS

Because they are briefly used and must be treated functionally to bear the flow of traffic, hallways frequently become the stepchildren of a home's over-all scheme. However, they can and should be treated

with decorative significance. In fact, decoratively speaking, the front hall is your calling card and should give some indication of what the rest of the house is like—contemporary or traditional, simple or ornate, formal or informal. Even in the postage-stamp-size foyer where there's no room for furniture, a specific

**The front hall gives that important first impression and should be decorated with care.**

A small entrance like this one can be enlivened by one or two unusual accent pieces.

decorating theme can be established in your choice of flooring, wallcovering, window treatment, lighting fixtures, mirror frame, or other accessories.

At first glance, the dimensions of all-too-many hallways seem inadequate for conveying a promise of spaciousness throughout the rooms beyond, but lack of square footage can usually be overcome by the use of decorating techniques that fool the eye into seeing more. Here are some of them:

**Tricks with mirrors.** A large mirror on the wall will convey an illusion of depth to the smallest anteroom. Even more effective is the use of a mirror that covers one wall and doubles the size of a half-round or rectangular table placed strategically in front of it.

**Scenic wallpaper.** Outdoor scenes seem to push back the wall, taking the eye down a garden path or along a quaint street. Only one wall need be covered with the scenic paper, while other walls can be painted or papered to match its background color.

**Coordinating floor and wall treatment.** An unbroken vista is more pleasing to the eye and gives an illusion of more space in a small area. Choose a light or neutral tone for the flooring, then have the walls and ceiling painted to match it. Parallel lines will also guide the eye into seeing more space than is actually there. For example, have strips of a wood-grain inset laid in the floor, then continue them on up one wall.

**Making a small window seem larger.** A window might well be the focal point of a hall and the means of suggesting the decorating character of the rooms beyond. To increase the size and importance of a window, hang curtains from the wall on either side rather than covering the window only, or add on to the existing window with a shadowbox, valance, or other architectural feature. A tailored window shade will suggest a simple contemporary interior, Austrian shades hint at formality, and cafe curtains in a provincial print give promise of a country look. If the window has a view of trees or greenery, repeat this look inside with plants.

A built-in bookcase and cabinet is one way of eliminating wasted space in a hallway.

Since there is seldom either the floor space or the need for more than one or two items, hall furniture comes in the category of accent pieces. This means furniture that has some outstanding decorative feature to command attention—an interestingly shaped chair, a table with an unusual base, a chest of drawers with beautiful hardware, or an upholstery fabric in a particularly lovely color.

The attic often reveals a forgotten treasure that will perk up an entrance hall. Definitely not to be shoved out in the hall as is, however, are the battered settee, the dining chair that's literally on its last legs, and the rickety end table that had to be replaced. If the defects of these pieces were obvious in a whole roomful of furniture, they will stand out even more when displayed alone.

You can, on the other hand, achieve a splendid and economical decorating victory by redoing an old piece of furniture. Painting an old chest of drawers in a zingy accent color and changing the hardware may produce an effect you couldn't achieve with something newly purchased. An old deacon's bench might need nothing more than a refinishing and new seat pad to recapture its charm. As for the one-of-a-kind relic that never found its niche—an Edwardian rattan chair or Victorian marble-topped table, perhaps—the hallway of your traditionally decorated home may be just the right spot at last.

When buying a piece of furniture for the entrance hall, always have scale uppermost in your mind. If the hallway is small or narrow, it may be best to decide on space-saving, wall-hung furniture that will not impede the flow of traffic. A narrow shelf, made decoratively important by hanging a mirror and pair of sconces over it, requires only inches of space and is an ideal substitute for the console table that would look awkward in close quarters. Work with a floor plan before you purchase anything. Since a hallway may have

several doors opening onto it, there's often less space than you think for placement of furniture.

Whether your hall is so small there is no place to put anything, or so large you want to dramatize its spaciousness with uncluttered simplicity, there are wonderful decorative effects to be achieved by accessorizing rather than furnishing.

Here is your chance to indulge a love for towering greenery, because plants are one of the most effective of all hall decorations. They provide a nice transition between outdoors and indoors, while at the same time linking the hall to the decor of the rest of the house. A Japanese bonsai is a sign of welcome into an Oriental atmosphere, lacy ferns hint at tradition, and pots of geraniums herald the casual country look.

Indoor trees and larger potted plants, when set directly onto the floor, emphasize its decorative appeal. Other items that can create the same effect are those unusual, charmingly off-beat accessories you may have often admired, but never quite knew how to utilize. For example, you might arrange a set of large glass bottles or urns on the floor, each repeating a different color from your flooring pattern. Similar arrangements can be made with old crocks in varied shapes and sizes, a set of natural or colored straw baskets, or an interesting pottery collection.

Utilizing the walls is another effective means of making people take favorable notice of your hallway. An art gallery in miniature can be created by covering an entire wall with pictures and three-dimensional objects. Wall-hung clocks and barometers, sconces, sculptured figures and planters, and displays of colored glass on shelves all make the entrance an area that will not go unnoticed.

Problems arise when the entrance is also a hallway, perhaps with a flight of stairs. Here we refer you back to the decorating tricks suggested in this chapter and in Chapter 4. High ceilings; narrowness, darkness, and cut-up wall surfaces are all listed, with suggested remedies; some of them are common knowledge, a few of them verging, as we said, on magic. But it might be emphasized that when strictly architectural difficulties are encountered, architectural devices such as dadoes, panels, and borders should be given consideration over color and pattern.

Of course, everyone wants the kind of home where visitors feel relaxed and welcome, and the place to start building this image is right at the front door. First of all, a visitor is grateful for the smooth execution of those tasks so often awkwardly handled by an unsure host—like disposing of hats, coats, parcels, and wet umbrellas. A guest can feel like an intruder when a frantic search fails to reveal a vacant coat hanger and there's no place to get rid of that dripping umbrella. These should be on every list of hall furnishings:

1. *Storage space.* It's essential to keep part of the hall closet, if you have one, free of clutter at all times. This is usually possible if you clear the interior seasonally, storing family belongings not in current use. When space simply can't be spared, or you don't have a closet at all, a decorative wall rack for hanging coats is an adequate substitute.

2. *Inclement weather necessities.* An umbrella stand and a storage box for overshoes can be kept in the closet when not in use so they won't be in the way—unless they are decorative enough to be an asset at all times. A chair or bench for removing overshoes is also appreciated. Where space is at a premium or a chair would ruin the decor, this need be no more than a folding stool, kept in the closet or borrowed from another room, or a narrow bench that slides under a hanging shelf-with-mirror arrangement that can be used for primping.

3. *A mirror and table.* Visitors like to make grand entrances, too. A place where they can set down purses and parcels while removing their hats and giving reassuring pats to hairdos is welcome.

4. *Good lighting.* Nothing adds as much warmth and good cheer to your greeting as the glow of light that surrounds you and your guests. A hall light fixture should be attractive to look at and fitted with bulbs that give sufficient brightness without glare. Where there's no table for a lamp, pole lamps and wall-hung or ceiling-hung fixtures are fine.

## ATTIC ROOMS

Since the days of the saltbox or the early Cape Cod, American homemakers have been faced with the problem of creating livable rooms amidst the slopes, slants, and gable ends of Colonial architecture. Although the situation is eased somewhat today by the full dormers and the skylights found in modern homes, decorating attic space still provides a challenge and a strong sense of reward.

The best approach is a direct one. Face the fact that you will be working with rooms in which walls and ceilings often merge, and abandon some of your standard precepts in favor of new thinking; or, borrow old ideas. A visit to the less pretentious homes in the restored village of Williamsburg, for instance, will show how expeditiously Colonial families dealt with this matter: they simply white-washed or calcimined the entire surface (except for the dark gleam of polished woodwork). Substituting paint for the long-ago

technique, this is still a good solution.

A visual merger of walls and ceiling can also be arranged by papering the room over-all in a pattern of tiny checks or diminutive florals. Because of their relatively low ceilings, attics can either seem cozy and intimate or closed-in and claustrophobic. Which effect you achieve depends upon how you handle decorating details.

As far as color schemes are concerned, because of natural light generally available, you can range over the entire spectrum for your choices. Choose a triad of primary colors; or try an analogous combination, such as yellow-green blending into green, blue-green, blue, and blue-violet. If you prefer monochromatic schemes, shade navy into royal into sky into baby blue. Another attractive scheme is light- and deep-toned pinks graduating into red against a background of white. Use color as a correction for the chopped-up look that occurs when too many roof lines cut into your room. Or use it simply for the joy of it, to bring life into your new playroom, guest room, child's bedroom, studio, or whatever you have designated as the new name for your attic. The following are other things that should be considered when decorating an attic area:

**Flooring.** Attics tend to "shrink" when ceilings are put in and the eaves closed off. For this reason, it's usually preferable to choose flooring in shades that are medium to light and that favor an over-all look, rather than flooring that features a pronounced pattern.

**Fabrics.** Informality is the keynote in attic rooms. Save your silks and satins for your downstairs drawing room; try for charm rather than elegance in your upstairs rooms. Denim, gingham, plaids, provincial prints, or old-fashioned cottons, such as sprigged muslins, will add big dividends to your decorating dollar.

**Furnishings.** Wear-weary tables and sagging sofas have no place in your newly renovated attic. If economy dictates the use of furniture that has seen better days, refurbish it with stain, paint, wallpaper, or even vinyl paper with the adhesive already on the back, to harmonize with your color scheme. If you're purchasing new furniture, the smaller-scaled designs are your best bet.

**Windows.** Particularly in older homes, attic windows often offer problems arising more from their position in the gable ends than from intrinsic lack of proportion. Better effects can be gained by treating the entire wall as an entity, than by dressing the window alone. Some of these effects follow.

Create a geometric design by outlining the peak of the wall with bright-colored molding, then making an arrangement of diamond-shaped and round picture frames above the window. Hang curtains to match the molding and accent the vertical line.

Highlight an odd-shaped end wall with paint bolder in tone than the other walls. Subordinate the window by the use of matching curtains. Tie this color accent to other walls with matching baseboards all around the room.

Paint the interior of a dormer to contrast with other walls, using a built-in window seat for comfort and a look of intimacy. Match or harmonize seat cushions with curtains.

Accent skylights with specially designed window shades covered in fabric to match your wallpaper.

Repeat the triangular effect by attaching a multi-armed painted Scandinavian sconce above the window. Repeat colors of sconce and candles in contemporary curtains. When employing an Early American theme, fasten a large American eagle above the window to fill the peak. Coordinate with a suitable Colonial print.

## BASEMENT AND GARAGE ROOMS

When designing basement rooms or those built in the garage area, apply the basic decorating rules you've used elsewhere in the house, but recognize the fact that renovations present special decorating challenges not typical of other areas. For example, a first step in planning rooms in a basement or garage with small windows is to determine how you'll dispel the darkness. Depending upon whether you prefer a contemporary or traditional interior, incorporate one or more of the following:

1. A backlit wall across one end of the room can be created by building a wall-to-wall plywood frame, then interspersing solid vertical panels with translucent ones of frosted glass, or shirred sheer curtains. A *shoji* screen works equally well. Light from behind.

Wood paneling and bright colors help give a warm feeling to a basement room.

2. Lamps and lighting fixtures, if used as the only source of light, should be more numerous than in the conventional room. Combine chandelier or other ceiling fixtures with sconces or wall fixtures. Be liberal, as well, with table or floor lamps.

3. White or light walls brighten a basement, but bright colors should be added to avoid a sterile white-washed look.

4. A "window" look can be created with wall recesses; fluorescent lighting shines through frosted or stained glass panes.

A cozy feeling is often as much psychological as physiological, so rely upon visual devices to produced a feeling of welcome and warmth. Color should be bold and positive. Neither the limited natural light afforded by basements, nor artificial light, brings out the best in pale, overly subtle hues. Heighten the attractiveness of light or neutral walls or floors with strong accent shades—scarlet, for instance, used with warm white; orange to brighten beige. The three primary colors are a good combination if you emphasize the reds and yellows more than the blues. Analogous schemes in the warm range are also effective, such as yellow, shading into yellow-orange, into orange, and finally, into red-orange.

Natural wood-grain walls help dispel a cold look in basements and garages. Use wood grains lavishly in the lighter tones, sparingly when the stain is dark. In

**The scarcity or lack of windows in a basement room make effective lighting a vital consideration.**

fabrics, textures such as corduroy or washable velveteen are more inviting than sleep-surfaced "warm" plastics or shiny glazed cottons. Bold, imaginative floor patterns show up to advantage in oversized basement or garage rooms.

Bold designs and colors in area rugs offer another means of getting greater warmth and decorative appeal into the basement room. For contemporary settings, there are abstract modern designs—sunbursts, geometric patterns, and sophisticated "op art" interpretations—that literally make a room come alive. The range of more traditional patterns is equally colorful and impressive, embracing bold florals and

familiar classic motifs.

In large basements or garages, "big" art is needed to break the broad expanse of walls. That small painting no longer used in your child's bedroom will look like a postage stamp if used in a room of generous dimensions unless you arrange other pictures along with it to form a grouping. Travel posters, decorative Japanese kites, or massive pieces of driftwood give you the scale you need. So, too, do examples of your children's grade-school art when enhanced with large, bright-colored mats.

Patterned slipcovers or curtains should feature strong, pronounced designs. In the basement, you can use the oversized hound's-tooth check, the big bold plaids, or the scaled-up chrysanthemums that you find too assertive for the rest of the house.

Beams, make-believe half-timbering, or dadoes around the wall add a feeling of intimacy to basement rooms. The boxlike dimensions of converted basement and garage rooms can be improved in various ways, particularly with built-in architectural details. Try breaking up one of your long walls with vertical columns, shelving, or wall-hung furniture. Or build two closets in opposing corners and join them with a bench fitted to the recess. A storage wall, with cabinets and shelves in various depths and planes, also adds dimension. Small windows can be enlarged in scale by various devices:

1. To increase the apparent size of a window and give it architectural importance, frame it with wide, flat molding painted a bright commanding color; adorn the frame with eye-catching horse or pony brasses.

2. Attach a shaped valance or lambrequin above the window. Fasten a window box, abloom with fake flowers, below.

3. Use a straight felt valance that hangs long on each end.

4. Use a bright brass rod to support a very full cafe curtain that covers part of the wall as well as the window.

5. Trim a window—top and bottom—with the wide exterior molding usually used on Colonial doorways. Hang shutters reaching from top to bottom of the new molding.

# BRINGING THE outside in

## 13

With today's life style, there is no reason why patios, balconies, and other outdoor living areas shouldn't relate directly to the interior decorating theme of the home. It should be noted that in recent years, as more emphasis has been placed on extending personal and family activity outdoors, there has been an increased awareness of bringing the outdoors inside the home as well. Through tasteful decorating and mixing the outside with the interior theme, the result is a total living environment. No longer are you going outside when you go to the patio, but rather you are just going to another part of the house, and vice versa. In order to achieve this, it takes some basic planning and, of course, proper decorating techniques.

Just as it is important for each room in the home to have a purpose and follow a general decorative theme, so too, the patio, if it is to become more than just a place outside, must do the same. Probably the most common use of a patio is as the headquarters of the barbecue. Actually, the barbecue is an excellent family center, because young and old alike enjoy a cookout. Gazebos and cabanas are other ways of using a patio or terrace, and in colder climates you can enclose the patio or porch in glass and make use of it all year. The sheltered outdoor area can be used as a hobby center or as a small greenhouse.

Whatever use you'll be making of your patio or balcony, make certain to select furnishings that can withstand the weather. There are a number of outdoor furnishings that are colorful, with strong fabrics and lacings, which are both nice to look at and durable. Some are suitable for both interior and exterior use.

**Wicker furniture and an assortment of hanging and potted plants are most appropriate on a patio.**

Wicker furniture, for instance, is attracting attention today, not only for its delicate beauty, but for its endurance. In other words, wicker, which was once relegated to porch or patio, is now contributing a cherishable hand-crafted look to interior decorating, that mixes innocently with other furnishings. But, if

there are steady gusts of wind in your area, it might be best to consider the heavier redwood-type patio furnishings.

There are several ways in which the outside can be brought in. One method is by using some of the new wallcoverings that give an outdoor feeling. Another way, as suggested previously, is to use "outdoor" furnishings in areas such as the family room. But of all the methods, plant tie-ins are the best. In fact, plants are one of the most natural and effective ways to accessorize a home. Few accessories contribute so effectively to the natural charm and distinction of a house or apartment as do well-grown and well-placed house plants. Today's modern houses, with their vast expanses of glass, offer limitless possibilities for bold mass groupings that make a garden a colorful part of the interior. And those of you who live in the traditional type of house or apartment with considerably less window exposure can just as effectively cut the cloth to fit your particular needs. From the tremendous assortment of flowering and foliage plants that do well indoors, you can decorate as picturesquely or as boldly as you like in the windows most

**Flowered prints work well with houseplants hung in a window.**

(Above) Potted indoor trees have a marvelous effect on any room.

(Right) Try to vary the size, color, and shape of your plants.

suited to your purpose. Many of the plants now featured are a far cry from those of our grandparents' day, when the common rubber plant, the ubiquitous aspidistra with its stiff green leaves, or the Boston fern dominated the bay window or sun parlor.

Live plants are always preferable, but if you are or would like to be a plant-lover, but lack a green thumb; have a home that is too dark or drafty for plants; or just want to fill in and brighten up hard-to-decorate areas, don't despair—you can spruce up your abode with beautiful artificial houseplants. With a bit of ingenuity, your home can look like a veritable Garden of Eden. And lifelike artificial plants are not affected by heat, cold, or the lack of light.

If you enjoy the look of foliage, some of these decorating tips may be just right for your home:

-Group artificial plants of various sizes and shapes to camouflage ugly radiators or exposed air conditioners.

-Tall artificial plants can brighten up dark corners. Install back-lighting to cast romantic shadows on the walls at night.

-Decorate unused fireplaces with beautiful artificial

plant arrangements. These groupings can also be placed on the mantel when the fireplace is in use.

-Use artificial lifelike plants to decorate your vacation home and never worry about watering while you're away.

When selecting plants—real or artificial— choose varieties whose color, shape, size, and textures complement one another. When the size of the planter permits, use low-growing, bushy specimens at the borders, placing increasingly taller plants to the rear. If the planter is open on more than one side, the lowest plants should be set around the perimeter, with the taller ones to the center. A corner calls for a tall plant such as an areca palm. Try a full fern on a coffee table, or a boxwood arrangement on a windowsill. In any case, remember that greenery adds a refreshing touch to any room and looks right with every style of furnishing.

As mentioned in Chapter 5, plants can be used in any room of the home—except possibly the children's rooms. In fact, plants are never out of place. They add that extra something to make a room more inviting and more alive. Plants do give a home a look

148

of vitality and realism, as well as help to unite the outside with the inside. And plants and greenery fit well with any decor—contemporary or traditional.

**Both flowering and foliage plants complement almost any room of the house.**

# PUTTING YOUR DESIGN PLANS
# together

## 14

Designing our homes is the most artistically creative activity available to most of us. Few of us are painters, writers, or musicians, but all of us live in homes that we can mold to reflect our tastes and interests. Our rooms are creative media through which we can express our own individuality.

Every individual has taste. It's a word that is almost impossible to define because it is so personal. The road to satisfying design begins with determining just what your taste (or preference) is in furnishings. If yours is an elegant way of life which includes formal entertaining, you will probably be most happy with traditional decor. If you live a casual, informal life, full of buffet suppers, family hobbies, and friends who "drop in," then the sophistication and simplicity of a contemporary home may be your favorite. Provincial homes are usually liked best by those who want a warm and friendly atmosphere, a touch of nostalgia, and refuge from the frantic world.

Of course, you can "mix" styles as well. Many well-known designers prefer the eclectic look, the combination of modern with traditional styles, even though everything in a room is spanking new. It's easiest to do when there's a unifying factor to a room. A room with tones and shades of a single color in upholstery, carpeting, walls, and draperies, can use a great variation of furniture styles in different wood tones. Another way to achieve an eclectic look is by selecting furniture that is compatible in styling. For example, most modern and Oriental blend nicely because of their similar straight lines; and since furnishings from some periods were inspired by those

of earlier cultures, they often combine unexpectedly well. Thomas Chippendale, for example, was enamored of the Orient, so his traditional English furniture mates magically with Oriental or with modern. Sometimes the materials that the furniture is made of will provide the unifying effect. Cane, for example, was used in 18th-century France, yet it is equally at home with modern. So go ahead and choose modern tables to mate with your Provincial pierced-back chairs. Rooms can span centuries and continents as well as

**(Above) Make designing your home your own work of art.**

generations in a family.

In the past few years, a new decorative form, known as "new country," has made an appearance. It is a blend of contemporary and traditional furnishings. The big, barny house, repainted in dairy colors, becomes light and airy and free. The architecturally uninteresting apartment, repainted in barn reds with fake beam ceilings added for a rustic touch, grows hospitable and homey. New country is different from Provincial because it isn't confined to French or Italian, and distinguished from Colonial because it isn't made up of love seats and rockers and braided rugs. So, you'll be able to mix a wing chair and butler's tray table with a mobile bar and modern wall stacks.

Rarely do people buy everything for their home at one time. There are the hand-me-downs for singles and newlyweds, the make-overs for growing families, and the family pieces dear to older couples who are moving to cozier quarters. A comfortable chair, a treasured family heirloom, an Oriental rug, even a collection of family pictures give warmth and originality to a room. But remember that when planning an eclectic scheme, select the best, not second rate. It's a mellow blending of decorating styles.

It must be remembered that furniture, like people, changes and mellows with age. It can last many years in many places, playing many different roles in many different rooms. Today's furniture is designed for change—for use today, as well as tomorrow. Today's dining room buffet is part of tommorow's children's-room furniture, and later, that child may well take that piece into his or her very own home. Both traditional furniture and modern furniture are made to serve more than one purpose, to show different faces in different settings. Buying multipurpose furniture stretches budgets and stretches space. For example, there's the dining chair that's light enough to be carried into the living room when there are extra guests, or the desk in the living room that's roomy enough for a buffet set-up. Or what about an end table that's really a nest of tables, so one or two can be placed in front of guests for snacks? A glass table on wheels can become a bar cart, and a sofa can become a bed for overnight guests.

And then there's the forerunner of them all—the modular wall system. Wall units are the original furniture magicians, revealing and concealing, turning themselves in the wink of an eye into a playroom, dining room, or hobby room. These modular systems are composed of open shelves, glass doors, wood doors, drawers, and cane doors. They hold everything—and do everything. Although modular furni-

A perfect example of a modular wall unit used in the living room.

ture is a product of 20th-century thinking, it can take 18th-century design, so lovers of tradition can buy contemporary functionalism with country styling. Units with cornices, moldings, and carvings in rich chateau woods can hold collections of clothing or antiques or books. These modern and traditional wall units can even move from room to room as life styles and needs change.

Remember that rooms are primarily to be lived in and used. Traditionally, the function of decorating has been to enrich our surroundings and to give us a sense of comfort. To be sure, this is still its major function. Today, however, decorating has assumed wider significance. Many of us live in homes and apartments that are poor in the design of space, have little architectural interest, and are difficult to organize. Decorating has become the means by which these deficiencies in our homes can be corrected. Consider these points: through proper furniture placement, decorating can make poorly planned rooms perform efficiently; through good use of color and pattern, it can make badly proportioned rooms seem larger or smaller; and through wise selection of furniture, it can make cramped space function as if it were generous.

The best way to start putting a decorating project all together is to study the interior architecture of the room or area to be furnished. Often, minor changes—a bolder cornice at the ceiling line, the addition of several electrical outlets, cutting a new or closing an existing door—can make all the difference in how livable the room will be. Sometimes, however, you can't see the forest for the trees, particularly if the room is very familiar. Draw back, take stock, and try to be objective. Examine each area individually: walls, windows, wood trim, lighting, hardware, floors, and adjoining rooms. Ask yourself, "Wouldn't it be better if ...?" and jot down proposed changes.

If you're going to be a short-term occupant of the room or home (if you rent and have a short lease),

you'll have to stifle the impulse to make any major architectural changes. Instead, work out ways to redecorate with paint, fabrics, and wallpaper. Color and pattern can minimize many flaws. Invest in furniture and accessories that will fit easily into another apartment or home should you move.

If you own your home or have a long-term lease, you'll find that correcting major architectural flaws will always be worthwhile. (If you rent, be sure to check the lease to be sure such changes can be made, and remember that once architectural changes are made in a rented unit, they usually cannot be removed when you move.) An irritating jog in a wall, or an ugly fireplace will stick out like a sore thumb (to you)—while the addition of one perfect detail, like a Colonial mantel that completes the mood of the room, will pull all your efforts together with one lovely, harmonious touch.

If you're going to add beams or paneling, or a chair rail and dado, now's the time. If these are already installed, you may wish to paint or bleach them. Or, you may want to make only a simple change—a few deco-

rative shelves, or one new door.

Get the feeling of each room. Walk around, and study it from every angle. If you don't have any furniture, take a grocery carton or barrel and place it where a couch would be. Sit down, and imagine Sunday night supper by the fire, or a teen-age record and pizza party. Look at the windows and consider the exposure. Walk in and out of the doors to get the feel of how the traffic flows.

As mentioned previously, your color scheme will generally be based on colors found in your upholstery, fabric, carpeting, flooring, walls (via paint and wallpaper), or accessories. To achieve the right balance of color and texture, study some successful rooms on pages 25 to 40. For a detailed discussion on the selection and effects of color and texture, see Chapter 2.

Of course, no truly personal home is ever finished, in the sense that decorating is never really at an end. You'll add a piece here, discard a piece there, and rearrange to suit your changing taste and family needs. The most important thing about this is that you're making the changes—and your plans should reflect your family's interests and personality. To accomplish this, make an analysis of the room or rooms you plan to decorate.

### Analysis of A Room

When analyzing a room, use a reporter's basic technique. That is, "interview" each room to find out exactly how it works and what you would like to change.

*Who* uses this room?

*When* is it used? At what times of day; in what seasons?

*Where* is the room located in relation to other rooms?

The location of a room affects traffic patterns; if the space is used as a thoroughfare, bear that in mind when you plan furniture arrangements and select floor coverings. The interrelation of rooms also af-

fects the decor. Unless you love visual surprises, you'll want rooms to relate to the adjacent spaces in terms of color and styles. Think of your home as a total environment, so that even if you redo only one or two areas now, you can plan ahead and end up with a cohesive whole.

*Why* do you want to change the decor? This question helps you identify not only what doesn't work about a room as it is now, but also what elements don't please you aesthetically, or are worn out and in need of replacement.

*What* elements will remain the same? This question clues you in to what you already have that could be the basis of a new scheme—antiques or art, perhaps. If you love to read and own a lot of books, consider making them the focal point by adding a wall unit. Don't discard anything until you have envisioned it with a fresh coat of paint or new fabric. Reupholstering your sofa and occasional chairs could be the start of a crisp, yet sophisticated room. Also, if you suddenly decide to replace your overstuffed sofa and armchairs with carpeted platforms and modular seating, be sure that the rest of the family shares your enthusiasm; otherwise, you may find yourself seated all alone under the track lights while they lounge in a bedroom watching TV. Remember that as your awareness of interior decorating increases, your taste will evolve, and you may eventually decide to get rid of some of the furniture you now have. Always be sure, however, that you are discarding something because you have decided it no longer fits in, not because fashion or the neighbors say it's not *a la mode*. Unless your first—and last—thought in decorating is what you like and relate to, you'll never feel at ease in your home.

The following checklist will assist you in analyzing your taste and relating it to your space and lifestyle. Richard Ryan of Bloomingdale's, New York, and the

**Dining area just right for two.**

editors of *House Beautiful's Home Decorating* (a Hearst publication) compiled it based on questions a designer might ask you. If you're uncertain about your answers, try Ryan's suggestion: for two weeks, keep a daily journal in which you record everything you do in your home, where you do it, and what space and equipment it requires. Ask other family members to contribute a list of their activities. Then, return to your study area and answer the questions you were unsure about.

YOUR HOME

**Type of Dwelling**

House          Apartment          Other

**Occupants**

**Adults**_____Age _____
_____Age _____
Children _____Age _____
_____Age _____
Are children living at home or away? _____
Pets _____
Other _____

**Special Considerations**

Invalid or elderly person_____
Large or unusual pets_____
Someone with allergies_____
Other _____
Domestic Help: Full-time _____
     Part-time _____ Services they
     perform _____
Maintenance duties performed by family members
_____

YOUR LIFE STYLE

Your family's everyday life is basically casual _____
_____formal_____
Family works/plays outdoors often _____
     occasionally _____seldom _____
House is used year 'round _____
     weekends _____vacations _____
     spring _____summer _____
     fall _____winter _____
Most evenings, the family is at home _____
     out _____

Family members travel often _____
     occasionally _____seldom _____

**Privacy and Togetherness**

Does every family member have a room of his own?
If not, are there places where each can be alone to rest, dream, pursue private activities? _____
Are there places furnished so that the whole family can enoy meals, games, conversations together?
_____

**Guests**

Is there space for overnight guests? _____
Could you create it by adding a convertible sofa to an existing space? _____

**Work**

Does someone work at home full-time? _____
Is there a home office now? _____
Could home office perform an additional function (e.g. dining area)? _____
Is there an area for part-time work such as menu planning, paying bills? _____
Do children have a place for doing their school work? _____
Are these areas quiet? _____
Do they have ample light, ample storage space, a good work surface? _____

**Play**

Where do children play? _____
Is it furnished for rough-housing? _____
Is there ample storage space for games, toys, books?
_____
Is storage space accessible? _____
Do teenagers have area for entertaining without disturbing other family members? _____
Do adults have spot for relaxing, private conversations? _____

**Hobbies**

What hobbies are pursued? _____
What space do they require? _____
What special equipment? _____
Must it be set up at all times? _____
If it is packed away, is there ample storage space?
_____

Is storage space accessible? _____
Is there sufficient light? _____

## Music

Is music important to family? _____
Can it be enjoyed without disturbing non-listeners?
_____
What musical instruments are played? _____
Where are they played? _____
Does family listen to stereo? _____
Where does this take place? _____
Are there areas where you would like to put addition-
    al speakers? _____

## Television

Number of sets _____Location_____
Does family watch TV often? _____
Do you want set(s) hidden when not in use? _____

## Books

Do family members read a lot? _____
Where do they read? _____
Is there comfortable seating there? _____
Is there adequate light? _____
Do you have enough bookshelves? _____
Where could you add more? (e.g., hallways, stairways,
    corners) _____

## Telephone

How much time do family members spend talking on
    the telephone? _____
Number of Phones ____Location _____
Are seating, phone books, writing surface close by?
_____
If phones were relocated or additional sets installed
    could you then do a task (sort laundry, cook dinner)
    while talking? _____

## Dressing

What is family routine for using bathrooms in
    morning? _____
    before dinner? _____at bedtime? _____
Could you improve on routine by creating dressing
    space elsewhere? _____

## Dining

Does family eat together? _____ Where? ____

If not, where do adults eat? _____
    children? _____
Does dining area have another function when not in
    use for meals? _____
If you seldom use dining room, what other use could
    you find for it? (e.g., library, guest room) _____
Is kitchen convenient to dining area? _____
If not, could you relocate dining area to living room,
    den? _____

## Entertaining

Do you entertain? _____How often? _____
Is entertaining primarily social? _____
    for business? _____
Average number of guests _____
How do you entertain?  Luncheon _____
Cocktail parties _____Buffet suppers _____
Formal, sitdown dinners _____
Barbecues, informal gatherings _____
Other _____
For conversation, do you prefer intimate seating
    groups or one large area? _____
For dining, do you prefer one large table or several
    smaller ones? _____
Do size and shape of table(s) suit the dining space?
_____
Do you have enough extra seating? _____
If space, time, help, and money were no object, what
    kind of parties would you like to give? _____

## Style

Check styles you like:
    Traditional _____Contemporary _____
    Provincial _____Eclectic_____
    "Natural" look _____Oriental _____
    Other _____
If you checked "Traditional" list the periods you
    prefer _____
List antiques or special pieces you want to incorporate
    into a scheme _____

## Color

Do you like color? _____
Prefer bright color _____ pastels _____
    dark _____neutrals _____
List colors you like _____
    dislike _____
List colors you wear most often _____

## Texture

Check textures you like:
    Rough (corduroy, linen, wool) _____
    Soft (velvet, fur, mohair) _____
    Smooth (silk, satin, chintz) _____
    Crisp (cotton, denim) _____

## Pattern

Do you like prints? _____
What type?  Plaids _____Checks _____
    Geometrics _____Stripes _____
    Florals _____
What scale?  Large _____Small _____

## Furniture

Check preferences:
    Wood _____ light _____ dark _____
    Plastic _____Lucite _____
    Wicker _____Bamboo _____
    Brass _____Chrome _____
    Lacquered _____Upholstered _____
    Other _____

## Windows

Is there a good view? _____ no view? _____
Is privacy a consideration? _____
Are any windows also doors? _____
Check preferences:  Shades _____ Draperies ____
    Shutters _____Venetian blinds _____
    Vertical blinds _____Other _____

## Floors

Is easy maintenance important? _____
Is area heavily trafficked? _____
Are existing floors in good shape? _____
Check preferences:  Wood _____
    Tile (ceramic, quarry) _____
    Brick _____Vinyl flooring _____
    Painted _____Stenciled _____
    Area rugs _____Broadloom _____
    Straw _____Shag _____
    Rya _____Oriental _____
    Wall-to-wall carpeting _____

## Walls

Check preferences:  Paint _____ Wallpaper ____
    Fabric _____Wood paneling _____
    Mirror _____Other _____

## Ceilings

Check preferences:
    Painted to match walls_____
    Painted to match woodwork _____
    Painted in contrasting tones _____
    Wallpapered _____
    Tented with fabric _____
    Beamed _____

## LIGHTING

Check preferences:
    All-over light _____Indirect _____
    Pools of light for accent _____
    Candlelight _____
For everyday, what kind of light do you require for
    reading? _____working? _____
    relaxing? _____
    cooking? _____
For entertaining, what kind of light do you like? __
Check preferences:  Lamps _____
    Wall or ceiling fixtures _____
    Track lighting _____
    Spots (up-and-down lighting) _____
During the day, how much natural light does room
    get? _____
Do you need special lights for growing plants? ____

## ACCESSORIES

Do you like lots of plants and flowers? _____
Do you have collections you want to display? _____
    What are they? _____
Do you have paintings or sculpture you would like to
    feature? _____
Do you have lots of books? _____
List all objects d'art, bibelots that are important
    to you _____
Could you build a scheme around any of your favorite
    things? _____

## BUDGET

Any professional will tell you that budget is just about
the most important item on your decorating agenda.
It determines what you can do with the space in the
time you have. Establishing and allocating a budget is
a personal matter, intimately connected with your
sense of values. Maybe you'd prefer air conditioning
to a new sofa, and would therefore be willing to re-
upholster the old one for now. Don't forget that a

large portion of your budget may go toward the "hidden" costs of decorating: technical necessities (plumbing, rewiring) and labor (painters, carpenters). To help focus on what's most important to you, consider the following points:

Do you own or rent? _____(For renters, mobile pieces are a better investment than built-ins.)

How long do you plan to live where you are now?
_____

Do you plan to add to your family? _____
_____

Will children be leaving home within the next few years? _____

Do you require that your scheme be completed now, or are you willing to add to it over time? _____

How much do you intend to spend now on decorating? _____
over the next year? _____ five years? _____

## Putting It All on Paper

Now that you've got the feel of the room or rooms, and all the interior architectural changes have been decided, it's time to get it all together on an exact room floor plan. Without a floor plan, you're apt to run into the aesthetic problem of poor balance and the more practical problem of traffic jams. You may also find, to your dismay, that your chairs fit in fine around the dining table but there isn't enough room to pull them out comfortably to seat eight people. Or, the hutch you planned to place between the two windows is just a couple of inches too long—and there's no place else to put it. Such headaches can be avoided when you plan on paper before you buy.

To make the task of drawing a floor plan simpler, buy some graph paper that's marked off into ¼-inch squares. Then draw on one of the sheets the dimensions of your room to a scale of ¼-inch equals one foot. In the appropriate places, mark off windows, projecting beams, and doors. Indicate by drawing an arc how far each door will swing out into the room. Using the sample furniture outlines also included in this chapter, and drawn to the same scale, trace the outlines of the furniture you own or plan to buy on craft paper and cut them out.

If you want to make your plan three-dimensional, add walls. Three walls, rather than four, will enable you to look in for a better view if you back your graph paper with cardboard and stand the walls around the floor in cube fashion. You can also have four walls, laying them flat around the floor like a box taken apart, and using your imagination to complete the

picture. Either way, you will be able to get a better perspective on everything. Penciling in the dimensions of windows and doors and the wall space occupied by your furniture provides a fairly accurate picture of balance and scale relationships.

The size of your home and your very individual life style determines just how much furniture you need in each room and exactly how it's placed. Years ago, the fireplace was the center of interest in every room. Now you have a choice of what your focal point may be. It may still be the fireplace, but it could also be a conversation area built around a bay window. It may be a prized painting or a precious Oriental rug or a splendid wall system. Rooms should always be arranged by function, and there can be both major and minor focal points in a very large room. Small rooms tend to look best if the furniture is placed around the perimeter of the room, with the center area free of clutter. In large rooms, the furniture arrangement can be more flexible.

When making any arrangement, note the traffic lanes in and around furniture groupings. Nothing is more awkward than having to shift your chair when someone wants to open the refrigerator or buffet door; or to have a conversation or television viewing repeatedly interrupted by people walking back and forth between you and what you are facing. A so-called conversational seating arrangement should group sofa and chairs close enough for friendly chatting, leaving space for others to walk around, not through it. Where drawers or doors must be opened, there should be enough space for the person to stand in front of them without obstructing anything. As a general rule, through-traffic lanes should be at least 2 feet wide. Leave about a 3-foot clearance at all doorways, 4 feet at the front-door entrance.

But, before making your final arrangement, let's examine some of the basics in furniture placement. Long before color, pattern, and ornaments make their appearance, a well-balanced room must be planned for the common-sense function provided by the arrangement of its furniture. Maximum usefulness and comfort must be extracted from space large or small; groupings must be planned in relation to their particular purpose.

The chief guide in simplifying the arrangement of furniture is to plan your groupings in terms of activities. When you plan in this manner, you don't wonder, "Now where should I place the easy chair?" Instead, you ask, "Where should I locate the reading center?" Then, once you have decided upon an area for this activity, you haven't merely found a place for a chair, but for all the pieces that go to make up an integrated, functional grouping.

This rule may seem quite obvious. Nevertheless, many a decorator has had, for example, expensive built-in bookcases constructed along a wall without ever giving a fleeting thought to whether the study and reading centers, which depend for functionality upon this piece of furniture, can find a place nearby. They forget the elementary fact that pieces of furniture are intended to be used together, not in isolation. Thus, if music means a great deal to you, you may very well make the piano the focal point of the room and assign it the best location. Or this place may go to your television set or to your conversation grouping instead. Indeed, if the room is to express a highly decorative note, you may have it revolve about an exquisite piece of furniture—a breakfront cabinet, for instance—or even a highly prized oil painting.

Also, you should consider the room architecturally. What is its most beautiful feature? The hearth? The bookcase-lined walls? The window with a view? Perhaps it is that long uninterrupted wall space, ideal for the sofa grouping. Which do you wish to emphasize? If your room has no special handicaps to surmount, such as broken wall spaces, double crossings of traffic, difficult windows, or the off-center fireplace, then you can feature whichever area you choose for your most important furniture grouping and make it the center of interest.

**A beautiful fireplace could be the feature you wish to emphasize.**

Once you have allocated an activity to a particular area, the arranging of furniture within that grouping almost solves itself. Your grouping will not only be functional, but will express your individuality.

Decoratively, groupings should give the effect of completion. This is attained largely through producing an effect of equilibrium by the use of either bisymmetric or asymmetric balance.

Bisymmetric balance repeats the same pieces of furniture at equivalent positions on either side of an imaginary center axis. This balance is exactly divisible into two identical halves by the dotted horizontal center axis; one side exactly mirrors the other. This confers a feeling of unity and completion. Bisymmetric balance is sometimes referred to as formal balance, in the belief that it expresses a feeling of formality. Actually, however, balance is only one element in establishing a decorative effect. If the furniture, fabric, and accessories of a grouping are informal, then, despite bisymmetric balance, so is the over-all effect. With formal constituents, of course, the effect achieved will be formal.

Asymmetric balance, on the other hand, uses dissimilar constituents at unequal distances from a center axis. For instance, we may form a face-to-face conversation grouping which consists of a love seat on one side, and a pair of club chairs side by side on the other. This grouping not only gives the effect of completion that results from balance but it also may be more interesting than formalized bisymmetry.

In addition, the pieces in your grouping should be in scale with one another. Thus, a delicate end table alongside an oversized sofa errs with respect to scale. Or a slender lamp upon a large table errs similarly.

Scale applies not only to mass, but to height. Often, by building up a grouping vertically, you endow it with importance and beauty. Thus, wall decor such as

This arrangement makes successful use of a corner area.

pictures and mirrors, should receive special thought, especially for use over relatively low horizontal pieces like sofas and unit cabinets. Also, pairing two small pieces together may help achieve proper scale where one piece alone might appear too skimpy and insignificant. Moreover, in grouping furniture, capitalize on your corners. Nothing detracts so much from the decor of a room as neglected corners. To neglect corners, in fact, is to sacrifice one of the most desirable architectural features of a room, one which can offer an effective backdrop for even your main centers of interest. But sticking a solitary occasional chair in a corner is no solution.

Corners particularly invite the use of unit and sectional furniture, which follow the angle of the wall. Such pieces, too, offer more possibilities for interesting arrangement. You may even find it desirable to cater-corner a small piece of furniture. Or you may plan a semi-circular grouping near a corner. Corners especially recommend themselves for such activities as studying, or as places for baby to play. So look to your corners for activity areas. They're useful, and add to a room's usefulness and good looks if you plan them so.

Just as each grouping should exhibit unity and variety, so should this be the effect of your room as a whole. This is possible only if all your groupings seem to belong together—to be parts of an integrated

whole. Such integration results through uniformity in furniture size, as well as through unity of color scheme, floor treatment, and decorative effect. From this standpoint, too, rooms must be in balance. The simplest way to check for over-all room balance is to divide the room into four quarters. Then you can see whether your layout utilizes each quarter equally. Thus, if you grouped most of your living room wood pieces in one section of the room, the result would be lack of balance. So it is with upholstered pieces, as well as with pattern and with a particular color.

If, moreover, you have a large breakfront cabinet against one long wall, you must build up the wall opposite it as well. This is another instance in which pictures or mirrors prove effective, as would ceiling-to-floor draperies. Of course, this injunction must take into account doors, arches, windows, and broken wall expanses. You should strive to make each quarter of your room of equal decorative importance. It promotes room harmony and interest.

Scale is a consideration in over-all decor as well. Furniture should not only be in scale within a grouping, but should be of a scale that suits the dimensions of your room; otherwise the room may become overcrowded, or lack sufficient space for the furniture, as occasionally happens in the selection of a console extension table intended for serving refreshments.

Overcrowding, obviously, is undesirable. If this is

your problem, keep in mind that you can transfer an activity to a less congested room. Thus, you can relieve congestion in the living room by setting up your television center in the family room or dining room, and so convert these areas into around-the-clock rooms. Guest bedrooms and dens similarly offer opportunity for conversion into dual-purpose rooms. Frequently, of course, trying a different arrangement will help to avoid overcrowding—like placing twin beds next to each other—head to foot—against a long wall instead of in a parallel position. In other cases, substitutions may be called for—a round instead of a rectangular dining table, a smaller sofa, one less chair, or an arrangement of wall-hung furniture to take the place of miscellaneous storage pieces.

Also, allot each grouping in the room an amount of space commensurate with its functional aspects and decorative importance. Leave space around each grouping to produce an effect of openness and to avoid obstructing room traffic or access to a closet or drawer. In line with this, don't obstruct a pleasant outdoor view. Instead, use low pieces of furniture in your window groups as well as draw draperies.

Sometimes it is good to make several floor plans. If this seems to be a duplication of effort, remember there is more than one way to solve a problem. Often, by trying out the various possibilities, both advantages and disadvantages not obvious at first may come to your attention.

Don't underestimate the importance of working out the best possible floor plan for each of the active rooms in your home. A small amount of work in the planning stage may eliminate years of discomfort and dissatisfaction in the future. And once your chart or plan is arranged to suit you, you have a basic guide to work from. This is your own "blueprint"—so keep it with you as you continue to select, and eliminate lost time and worry.

**Swatch Cards**

You have your room plans. You know where everything is, how big it is, and where everything is going. Now you get to the frosting on the cake—fabric, wallpaper, paint, rugs, furniture. Unless you're an unusual person it's awfully hard to carry color and pattern and design in your head; so, we suggest that you make a swatch card for each room or area that you're finishing.

A swatch card is simply a piece of cardboard to which you attach samples of fabric, paint chips, wall-

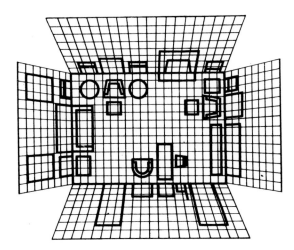

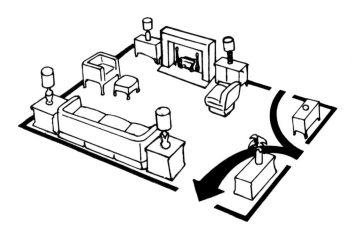

**A flat floor plan on a squared grid is shown at left, while a 3-D type is illustrated at right. The squared grid is one of the most popular methods of laying out a floor plan. The sizes and template shapes of popular furniture pieces are given on pages 160 to 163. Standard window and door sizes are also noted. Once the scale is determined, measure your room and mark off the appropriate number of blocks on the squared grid. Then indicate all permanent features: doors, windows, and fireplaces. Other elements should also be taken into consideration. Next, copy on paper and cut out the proper furniture templates. Now you're ready to begin moving furniture on the paper—experiment with the arrangements until you find the one you like best.**

paper, carpeting—whatever you're using in a particular room. With it all laid out before you, you can easily see if your choices are harmonious and vibrant, or if they fight and make you jumpy. This saves costly, nerve-wracking mistakes. If you start your swatch card with just paint and/or fabric, you can make sure that the other things are chosen to match. Do look at all colors in daylight as well as artificial light—and remember that wall color will be intensified because the walls reflect each other.

We mentioned magazine clippings in Chapter 1. As you plan, you'll find pictures of rooms, or shutters, or a hooked rug pattern that you like—or perhaps a chandelier, or old French copper *au gratin* pans, or a wrought-iron planter that you love. If possible keep a folder or file of the clippings. Then, when you're shopping for just the right thing, you have a point of reference.

Now that your careful plan is compiled, you're ready to act. You'll find that this thorough groundwork will be very profitable when you actually get into the exciting business of buying furniture and ordering fabric. Actually, today's homemaker is faced with a unique problem when decorating. The wealth

of merchandise in all price categories that awaits a person, the variety of decorating styles in vogue, and the never-ending succession of new and improved products being created can make it difficult for a person to make up his or her mind.

Knowledge is the key to ending one's doubts and confusion. A little "arm-chair" shopping is invaluable in acquiring the confidence necessary to make the right decisions—and it's a lot easier on the feet than heading for the shopping center without a clear idea of what it is you are really after. Before making any large purchase, you undoubtedly study the advertisements to check prices, then scan magazines and newspapers to learn about the latest developments in the product. Finally, you decide which brand best suits your needs.

Furnishing a home requires much the same approach. To use this book as it was intended, acquire the habit of looking before you leap into any decorating project. Try to see the finished room in your mind's eye, then set out to build it step by step. The more generous you are with your time in planning purchases now, the greater will be your enjoyment later.

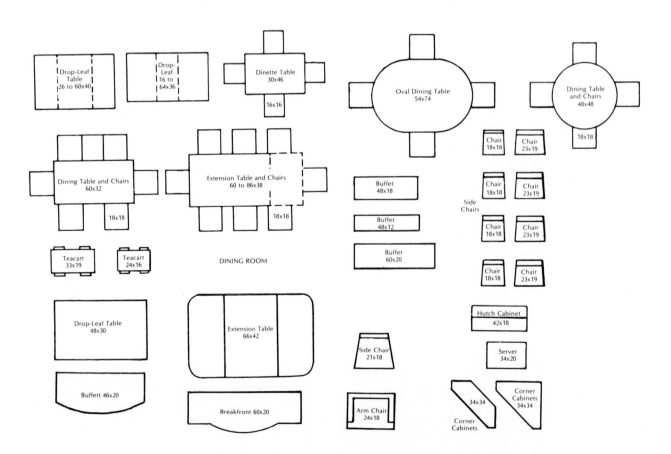

SEATING & STORAGE FURNITURE

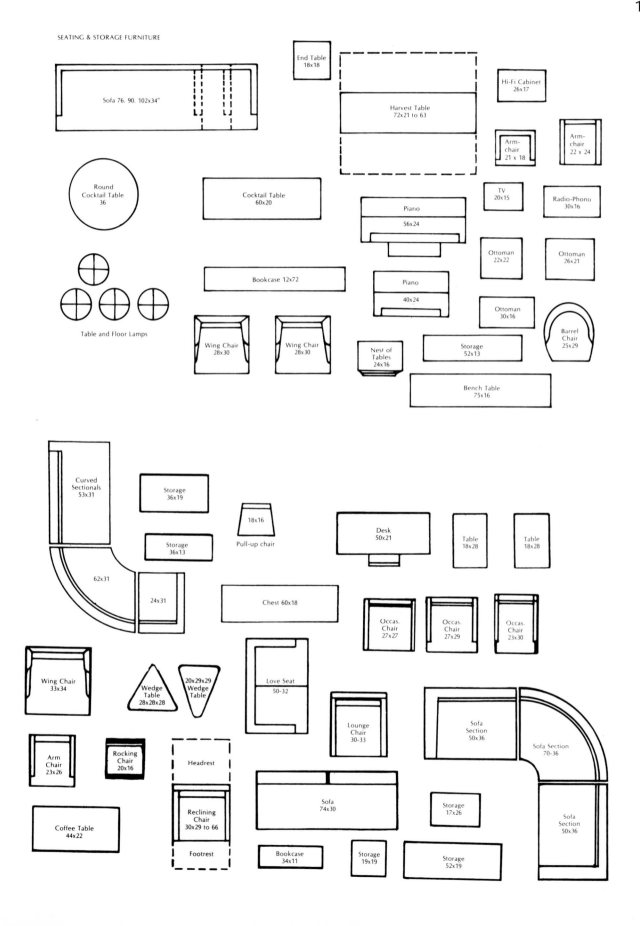

Sofa 76. 90. 102x34"

End Table
18x18

Harvest Table
72x21 to 63

Hi-Fi Cabinet
26x17

Arm-
chair
21 x 18

Arm-
chair
22 x 24

Round
Cocktail Table
36

Cocktail Table
60x20

Piano
56x24

TV
20x15

Radio-Phono
30x16

Ottoman
22x22

Ottoman
26x21

Bookcase 12x72

Piano
40x24

Ottoman
30x16

Table and Floor Lamps

Wing Chair
28x30

Wing Chair
28x30

Nest of
Tables
24x16

Storage
52x13

Barrel
Chair
25x29

Bench Table
75x16

Curved
Sectionals
53x31

Storage
36x19

18x16

Pull-up chair

Desk
50x21

Table
18x28

Table
18x28

Storage
36x13

62x31

24x31

Chest 60x18

Occas.
Chair
27x27

Occas.
Chair
27x29

Occas.
Chair
23x30

Wing Chair
33x34

Wedge
Table
28x28x28

20x29x29
Wedge
Table

Love Seat
50-32

Lounge
Chair
30-33

Sofa
Section
50x36

Sofa Section
70-36

Arm
Chair
23x26

Rocking
Chair
20x16

Headrest

Reclining
Chair
30x29 to 66

Footrest

Sofa
74x30

Storage
17x26

Sofa
Section
50x36

Coffee Table
44x22

Bookcase
34x11

Storage
19x19

Storage
52x19

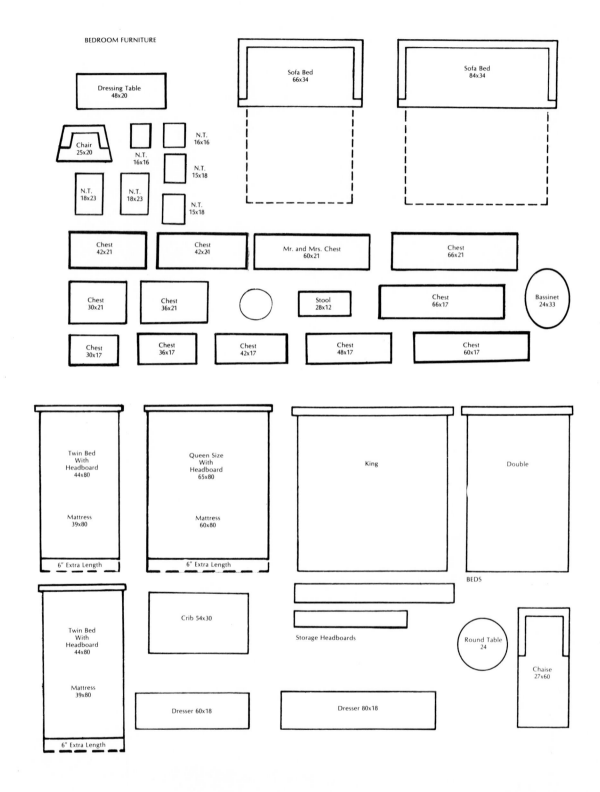

BEDROOM FURNITURE

Dressing Table
48x20

Chair
25x20

N.T.
16x16

N.T.
16x16

N.T.
16x16

N.T.
15x18

N.T.
18x23

N.T.
18x23

N.T.
15x18

Sofa Bed
66x34

Sofa Bed
84x34

Chest
42x21

Chest
42x21

Mr. and Mrs. Chest
60x21

Chest
66x21

Chest
30x21

Chest
36x21

Stool
28x12

Chest
66x17

Bassinet
24x33

Chest
30x17

Chest
36x17

Chest
42x17

Chest
48x17

Chest
60x17

Twin Bed
With
Headboard
44x80

Mattress
39x80

6" Extra Length

Queen Size
With
Headboard
65x80

Mattress
60x80

6" Extra Length

King

Double

BEDS

Twin Bed
With
Headboard
44x80

Mattress
39x80

6" Extra Length

Crib 54x30

Storage Headboards

Round Table
24

Chaise
27x60

Dresser 60x18

Dresser 80x18

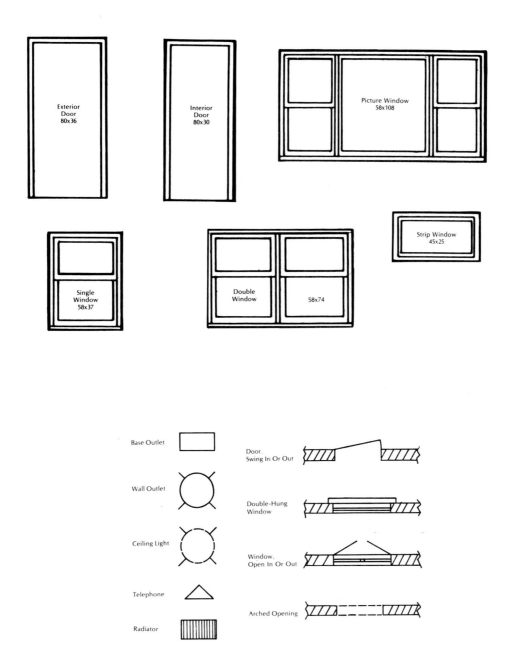

Exterior Door 80x36

Interior Door 80x30

Picture Window 58x108

Single Window 58x37

Double Window 58x74

Strip Window 45x25

Base Outlet

Wall Outlet

Ceiling Light

Telephone

Radiator

Door. Swing In Or Out

Double-Hung Window

Window. Open In Or Out

Arched Opening

# Index